Native American Biographies

JIM THORPE

LEGENDARY ATHLETE

Barbara Long

Enslow Publishers, Inc.

44 Fadem Road   PO Box 38
Box 699   Aldershot
Springfield, NJ 07081   Hants GU12 6BP
USA   UK

Library of Congress Cataloging-in-Publication Data

Long, Barbara, 1954-
    Jim Thorpe: legendary athelete / by Barbara Long.
      p. cm. — (Native American biographies)
    Includes bibliographical references and index.
    Summary: A biography of one of the greatest all-around athletes in
history, probably best-known for his record-breaking track and field
performance in the 1912 Olympic games.
    ISBN 0-89490-865-0
    1. Thorpe, Jim, 1887-1953—Juvenile literature. 2. Athletes—United
States—Biography—Juvenile literature. 3. Indians of North America—
Biography—Juvenile literature. [1. Thorpe, Jim, 1887-1953. 2. Athletes.
3. Indians of North America—Biography.]
I. Title II. Series
GV697.T5L66 1997
796'.092—dc20
[B]   96-9226
                                                                    CIP
                                                                    AC

Printed in the United States of America

10 9 8 7 6 5 4 3 2 1

Photo Credits: AP/Wide World Photos, pp. 85, 87; Archives &
Manuscripts Division of Oklahoma Historical Society, p. 23; Archives,
University of Illinois at Urbana-Champaign, John R. Case papers, pp. 6,
56; Barbara Long Associates, p. 96; Cumberland County Historical
Society and Hamilton Library, pp. 13, 35, 36, 45, 58, 89; National Football
League Properties, p. 82; UPI/Bettman, pp. 68, 69, 76.

Cover Photo: Jim Thorpe portrait by Paul Bloser, Cumberland County
Historical Society and Hamilton Library.

CONTENTS

Author's Note

James Francis Thorpe, a Sac and Fox Native American from Prague, Oklahoma, is probably best known for his record-breaking track and field performance in the 1912 Olympic games. He is also well known for his superior football talent. Thorpe's name is on the short and distinguished list of men who have played both professional baseball and professional football. Yet Jim Thorpe's athletic talent extended beyond track, football, and baseball. He was also skilled in basketball, swimming, golf, bowling, gymnastics, rowing, hockey, figure skating, billiards, hunting, fishing, horseback riding, dancing—just about any activity he tried.

Because Thorpe had amazing athletic talent, his story has grown to include some myths as well as facts. For example, one myth is that Thorpe did not train during his two-week ocean voyage to the 1912 Olympics. In fact, Thorpe trained very hard, as any Olympic athlete must. Indeed, a photograph shows Thorpe running on the USS *Finland* during its passage to Sweden. This book is based on facts about Jim Thorpe. The facts alone make Thorpe a legendary athlete.

— ◆ —

The 164 athletes representing the United States at the 1912 Olympic games received an especially warm welcome from the thirty thousand spectators.

An Olympic Star Is Born

The 1912 Olympic games opened on July 6 under sunny skies in Stockholm, Sweden. The hour-long ceremony began with a parade of athletes from the twenty-eight competing nations. As each athletic team entered the brand-new stadium, patriotic fans cheered their support. The 164 athletes representing the United States wore navy blue jackets, white pants, and straw hats. They received an especially warm welcome from the thirty thousand spectators. Despite the magnificent spectacle, an air of impatience could be felt from the crowd. They were anxious for the "real" show to begin.[1]

◈ 1912 Olympic Games ◈

One of the athletes waiting to compete in the 1912 Olympic games was Jim Thorpe. Thorpe, a Native American from the United States, was both strong and fast. At this opening ceremony, Thorpe was not well known to Olympic fans. His name was better known to American college football and track followers. By the closing ceremony of the Olympics, however, his name would be well known throughout the sports world.

◈ Pentathlon ◈

Jim Thorpe began setting Olympic records on Sunday, July 7, 1912. His first athletic contest was the pentathlon. This competition included five track and field events—the long jump, javelin throw, 200-meter race, discus throw, and 1,500-meter race. It was added to the 1912 games mainly through the efforts of the Swedish Olympic Committee. All-around contests such as the pentathlon were supposed to favor Scandinavian athletes. On the other hand, American athletes, who were often viewed as specialists, were not expected to do well in multi-event contests.

That Sunday, around 1 P.M., Thorpe prepared for the long jump. To place first, he needed to score better than 6.85 meters (22.47 feet).[2] This mark, made by Norway's Ferdinand Bie who was favored to win the pentathlon, was the best in the event so far. Thorpe began running about 9 meters (30 feet) from the take-off board. At the board he leaped into the air, landing 7.07 meters (23.19 feet) away. In his first event in his first-ever Olympic contest, Thorpe won first place.

The next event, the javelin throw, was not considered Thorpe's strongest. The first time he had ever thrown the long, wooden spear was just two months before the games. Yet Thorpe—with a throw of 46.71 meters (153.21 feet)—snared third place among the field of entrants.

The 200-meter race was a very close one. Thorpe crossed the finish line just 1/10 second ahead of two other Americans. His time of 22.9 seconds earned him another first place in a pentathlon event. Then Thorpe won the discus throw by launching the round, flat weight 35.75 meters (117.26 feet). The men's discus weighs 2 kilograms (4.41 pounds).

The final pentathlon event was the 1,500-meter race. Thorpe started off slowly, running in the next-to-the-outside lane of the track. In the middle of the second lap, with Bie leading, Thorpe began to pick up his pace. By the third lap, Thorpe was alongside Bie. By that time the Norwegian had spent most of his energy. Unable to push himself in front of Thorpe, Bie had to watch as Thorpe sped ahead of him. Thorpe won the race with a time of 4:44.8. Meanwhile, Bie fell behind several other runners and finished the race in sixth place.

With four first places and one third place—for a total of seven points—Jim Thorpe won the gold medal in the pentathlon. He also proved that Americans could be all-around athletes as well as specialists. Commenting on Thorpe's success, Commissioner James E. Sullivan of the American Olympic Committee said:

> *His all-around work was certainly sensational. It is a complete answer to the charge that is often made, that Americans specialize in athletics. In fact, the pentathlon was added to the games especially for the benefit of foreigners, but we have shown that we can produce all-around men, too. It also answers the allegation that most of our runners are of foreign parentage, for Thorpe is a real American, if there ever was one.* [3]

❖ A Real American ❖

As a Native American, Thorpe was indeed a "real" American. However, he was not officially an American citizen. Before the 1920s, not all Native Americans were recognized as United States citizens. Some Native Americans had citizenship rights through treaty agreements or special congressional acts. Not until 1924 did the United States Congress pass the Indian Citizenship Act. This gave United

States citizenship to every Native American born within the territorial limits of the United States.

The day after his pentathlon victory, Thorpe competed in the high jump event. He tied for fourth place with a mark of 1.87 meters (6.13 feet). Thorpe also placed seventh in the long jump, leaping 6.89 meters (22.60 feet).

❖ Decathlon ❖

On Saturday, July 13, Jim Thorpe began the grueling decathlon. This ten-event track and field competition, also added to the Olympics in 1912, is one of the toughest athletic contests in any sport. It serves as a test of endurance and all-around ability.

The decathlon began in a heavy downpour of rain, making the field conditions wet and slippery. On this day, three events—the 100-meter dash, the long jump, and the shot put—were held. Thorpe placed third in the 100-meter dash with a time of 11.2 seconds. The event was won by American sprinter E.L.R. Mercer, who finished in 11 seconds flat.

Due to the muddy ground, Thorpe slipped in the long jump. He was called for two faults before making a clean jump of 6.79 meters (22.27 feet). This effort earned him second place.

To clinch the lead at the end of the day, Thorpe needed a good showing in the shot put. He came through—heaving the 7-kilogram (16-pound) ball 12.89 meters (42.28 feet) to win the event. Based on his score, Thorpe's performance on that Saturday was not dampened by the rain. At the end of the day he led the other athletes in total number of points.

The next day dawned sunny, and, like the sun, Thorpe himself soon began to shine. He finished first in the high jump, leaping 1.87 meters (6.13 feet). Then, with a time of 52.2 seconds, he captured fourth place in the 400-meter run. Thorpe also won the 110-meter hurdles with a time of just 15.6 seconds. At the end of the second day, Thorpe again led the other athletes in total number of points.

Four events were scheduled for the third and final day of decathlon competition. Thorpe's mark, 36.98 meters (121.30 feet), in the discus throw earned him second place. Next Thorpe claimed third place in both the pole vault and javelin throw. After several days of strenuous competition, he should have been tired for the final decathlon event—the 1,500-meter race. Instead, Thorpe shaved off 4.7 seconds from his time set in the same event during the pentathlon just one week before. His time of 4:40.1 also won him the race.

With his outstanding all-around performance, Thorpe won the decathlon gold medal. He earned a total of 8,412 points out of a possible 10,000! Hugo Wieslander of Sweden finished second, but nearly 700 points behind Thorpe's total. Thorpe was the first United States athlete to win the decathlon; only nine others have won it since that time. The other

American decathlon winners include Harold Osborn, in 1924; James Bausch, in 1932; Glenn Morris, in 1936; Bob Mathias, in 1948 and 1952; Milton Campbell, in 1956; Rafer Johnson, in 1960; Bill Toomey, in 1968; Bruce Jenner, in 1976; and Dan O'Brien in 1996. Thorpe was also the first athlete to win both the pentathlon and decathlon Olympic events.

King Gustav V of Sweden presented Thorpe with his gold medals. Shaking Thorpe's hand, the king said, "You, sir, are the greatest athlete in the world." The twenty-four-year-old Thorpe responded simply, "Thanks, King."[4]

— ◈ —

An impressed King Gustav V presented Thorpe with his Olympic gold medals.

Some stories report that Thorpe was rude to King Gustav and that he did not want to be bothered accepting the medals.[5] These stories are not true. Years later Thorpe said that it was the proudest moment in his life.[6]

The 1912 Olympic games showcased Thorpe's track and field talents, giving the young athlete world-wide recognition. Yet Thorpe's athletic ability would continue to amaze spectators. Jim Thorpe would prove King Gustav's words true. He would become known as the "World's Greatest Athlete."

"Bright Path"

The man who was called "the greatest athlete in the world" by King Gustav V began his life in very humble surroundings. James Francis Thorpe was born in a one-room cabin on a horse ranch near Prague, Oklahoma. In 1882 Jim's father, Hiram P. Thorpe, married Jim's mother, Charlotte View. Charlotte was of French and Native American descent. But Thorpe's Sac and Fox roots were deeper than his mother's heritage.

◈ Family History ◈

Jim's grandfather, Hiram G. Thorpe, was an Irish American from Connecticut. In 1842 he was hired as a blacksmith on the Sac and Fox Reservation in Kansas. Hiram G. married *No-ten-o-quah* ("Wind Woman"), a descendant of Chief Black Hawk. Sources differ as to whether "Wind Woman" was the chief's niece or granddaughter.

Black Hawk was born in 1767 and became a famous Sac warrior at the age of fifteen. He lead many war campaigns against the Cherokee and Osage. In 1804 the Sac and Fox chiefs signed an agreement to turn over their land east of the Mississippi River to the United States. They did this in return for yearly cash payments. Black Hawk as well as others did not recognize this agreement. They did not believe the chiefs had the authority to sign such an agreement.[1]

Most Native Americans had little understanding of private ownership of land as conceived by white people.[2] Sometimes one band gave away land that belonged to another. The United States government viewed its treaties with Native Americans as legally binding. However, many of the treaties were broken as white settlers moved into areas that had been reserved for Native Americans. Consequently, many small, but fierce, wars broke out between Native Americans and United States troops.

After the War of 1812, in which Black Hawk joined the side of the British, the great warrior signed the Treaty of 1816. This agreement allowed the sale of some Sac and Fox lands. The people held on to some of their lands in Illinois. In 1831, after white settlers began to overrun Native American lands, Black Hawk urged his people to hold fast to their land, by fighting if necessary.[3] United States government troops went to the area and forced the Sac and Fox people to move west of the Mississippi River.

In 1832 Black Hawk returned to his homeland with about two thousand followers, of which at least fifty were warriors. His people were starving in their new home in Iowa, so they returned to Illinois to farm. Black Hawk sent a small group of men to talk with General Henry Atkinson, who led the United States troops in western Illinois. Some soldiers—afraid that the Native Americans were going to trick the troops and fight rather than talk—shot most of the men in the small party before any negotiation began. This act started the Black Hawk War.

At first the Native Americans were successful in defeating United States troops. But they soon suffered heavy losses from the better-armed soldiers. When help from other bands did not come, Black Hawk retreated. Again he suffered heavy losses. Over three hundred of the one thousand Native Americans were killed. Many were women and children. Black Hawk was eventually captured, and the Sac and Fox were forced to move from their land along the Mississippi River. The band moved from what is now Illinois and Iowa to a reservation on the Kansas prairie. In 1869 the United States government again moved the Sac and Fox, this time from Kansas to "Indian Territory" in present-day Oklahoma.

In 1833, after being freed from prison, Black Hawk went to Washington, D.C., to meet President Andrew Jackson. He also dictated the *Autobiography of Black Hawk,* which tells about Sac and Fox life and confrontation with white settlers. Black Hawk died in 1838 at the age of seventy-one. James Francis Thorpe was related to this famous Sac and Fox chief.

Among the Sac and Fox members moved by federal troops was Hiram G. Thorpe and his family. Just one generation before Hiram, the Sac and Fox people numbered forty-five hundred. At the time of their forced removal, that number dropped to four hundred. The Sac and Fox's new home was located on an 11-kilometer (17-mile) strip of land between the North Canadian and Cimarron rivers, in present-day Oklahoma.

Hiram G. Thorpe and "Wind Woman" had six children. Hiram P., Jim Thorpe's father, was born in 1850. He had more Native American features than Irish ones. With jet-black hair and bronze-colored skin, Hiram P. looked like his famous ancestor Black Hawk.[4] An independent man, he did not like reservation life.[5] So Hiram P. moved his family a short distance from the reservation and started a horse ranch.

Many Native Americans follow the custom of naming their children after a significant event. The event can occur either during the mother's pregnancy or after the baby's birth. Jim Thorpe was born around 6:30 A.M. on May 28, 1888. Looking out the window, Charlotte saw the path to the cabin glowing in bright sunlight. She decided to name her ten-pound son *Wa-tho-huck*, or "Bright Path." Charlotte, a Roman Catholic, insisted that her children be baptized and go to church.[6] So "Bright Path" was later christened James Francis. A baptismal record kept at the Oklahoma Historical Society indicates that Thorpe was christened on November 19, 1887. This document also cites Thorpe's birthdate as May 22, 1887. However, most sources use May 28, 1888, as the date of Thorpe's birth.

❖ Thorpe Has a Twin Brother ❖

On that day in May, Jim's twin brother, Charlie, was also born. Jim spent his early days playing with Charlie. The two boys were inseparable.[7] They fished, hunted, and played Native American games. In one game, similar to today's "Follow the Leader," players followed a leader who might climb trees, swim rivers, or run under horses.

Jim, like the rest of the family, also helped with chores on the horse ranch. He fed the livestock, and he learned how to rope and break in wild horses. Jim and Charlie also picked wild berries, fished, and hunted game for food. These chores helped Jim grow strong, brave, and quick.[8]

Nearly every Saturday, the Sac and Fox villagers gathered, often at the Thorpe ranch. They prepared food to be eaten during the day, and they competed in athletic contests such as sprinting, wrestling, swimming, high and long jump, and horseback riding. Hiram P., known as "Big Hiram," almost always won these contests. He taught his children the value of physical strength and the importance of sportsmanship and fair play.[9]

Jim remembered his father's physical strength with these words: "He could walk, ride, or run for days without ever showing the least sign of fatigue. Once, when we did not have enough horses to carry all our kill, my father slung a buck deer over each shoulder and carried them twenty miles to our home."[10]

Jim was also proud of his ancestor Black Hawk. As he grew older he learned more about this noble warrior. In later years he said, "I am no more proud of my career as an athlete than I am of the fact that I am a direct descendent of that noble warrior."[11]

◈ Reservation Schools ◈

During the late 1800s, admission to reservation schools was free, and all Native American children were required to attend. However, many families feared that the boarding schools—which taught only white people's customs—would cause the youngsters to forget their Native American heritage.[12] These families did not want to send their children to the reservation schools. But Hiram and Charlotte wanted their children to learn both cultures.[13] Also, Hiram could speak and write English, and he believed in education.[14]

So at age six, Jim and Charlie were sent to the Sac and Fox Agency School about 37 kilometers (23 miles) away. At the school, students were taught to live like white people. Only English was spoken; in fact, speaking a Native American language was forbidden. Students spent half their time studying and half their time learning a trade on the school farm or playing outside. They returned home to their parents just for holidays and summers.

Jim, an energetic boy, performed best when playing sports at the school.[15] He played "prairie baseball," which was like today's sandlot baseball. Charlie, smaller and quieter, was a good student.[16]

In May 1896, Hiram decided to take his eight-year-old sons on their first hunting trip. However, on the morning of the trip, Charlie had a fever. So Jim went hunting without his twin brother. On the last day of the three-day trip, Jim killed a buck with his first shot. Hiram told his son that the village would have a feast, in honor of his first kill, when they returned home. This was the Sac and Fox tradition.[17]

However, when Jim and his father returned home, they discovered that Charlie was very sick. He had pneumonia and had been taken to a hospital in a nearby town. Hiram and Jim rushed to see Charlie, but they were too late to see the boy one last time. Charlie died before they arrived at the hospital. The death of his twin brother affected Jim greatly. His schoolwork suffered; he even lost interest in sports.[18]

❖ Thorpe Runs Away ❖

Jim ran away from school many times; each time, his father made him return. Once, Hiram hitched the wagon to some horses to take Jim back to school. He dropped the young boy at the school's doorstep and headed home. Using the back door, Jim immediately left the school on foot. Taking shortcuts, Jim reduced the 37-kilometer (23-mile) trip to 29 kilometers (18 miles) and arrived home ahead of his father.

❖ Haskell Indian Junior College ❖

In the fall of 1898, hoping to discourage Jim from running away from school, Hiram sent his son to Haskell Indian Junior College.[19] The school was located in Lawrence, Kansas, and was 483 kilometers (300 miles) from the Thorpe ranch. The government-run school, which at the time enrolled more than one thousand Native American students, was based on the military system. Students wore uniforms and marched to classes. White people's customs were pushed on Native American youth, and discipline was

— ◈ —

As a teenager, Thorpe preferred outdoor play to classroom work at school.

heavily stressed. Feeling very lonely, eleven-year-old Jim turned to sports as a refuge.[20]

❖ Thorpe Turns to Sports ❖

Jim arrived at Haskell Indian Junior College on September 17, 1898. He saw his first football game in the fall of that year. The sport was becoming popular in America. Thorpe enjoyed watching the Haskell football team—especially Chauncey Archiquette, an outstanding Native American player.[21] One day Archiquette noticed Jim and began talking to the young boy. He made Jim a football from leather straps stuffed with rags. Soon Jim was organizing football games with other young boys at the school and beginning to overcome his loneliness.[22]

❖ Carlisle Indian School Football ❖

At Haskell, Jim had a chance to see the Carlisle Indian School football team. By this time the school—located in Carlisle, Pennsylvania—had a well-known athletic program, in large part due to the success of its football team. At the end of its 1899 season, the Carlisle football team accepted an invitation to play the University of California on Christmas day. Carlisle beat California, 2-0, in this "East-West" game. On its return trip home in January, the Carlisle team stopped in Kansas to visit the Haskell school. The Haskell students were proud that a Native American team had won the football contest.[23] To honor the Carlisle team, a special dress parade and inspection was held by the Haskell students.

One day, when Jim heard that his father was shot in a hunting accident, he left Haskell without permission. Unfortunately, he got on a train headed in the opposite direction of his home. After getting off the train, Jim ended up walking 435 kilometers (270 miles) to reach the Thorpe ranch. By the time he arrived home two weeks later, his father had recovered from the wound. However, just a few months later, his mother died from blood poisoning. Jim was very upset by his mother's death. As when Charlie died, he withdrew from people and activities; not even his father could reach him.[24]

❖ Thorpe Heads for Texas ❖

Jim did not return to Haskell, but remained on the ranch with his father. One day in 1901, Jim and his brother George went fishing, ignoring their ranch chores. When their father learned of their irresponsibility, he severely disciplined them. Jim ran away from home. He headed to Texas to find a job and show his father that he could be responsible.[25] At the time Jim was only thirteen years old. He was four feet eleven inches tall, and weighed 102 pounds. Still, he found work mending fences and taming wild horses.

When he had saved enough money, Jim bought a team of horses and returned to Oklahoma. Hiram was proud of his young son and very happy to have him home again.[26] For the next three years, Jim went to a one-room public school in Garden Grove. The school was just 5 kilometers (3 miles) from home.

During this time Jim also played baseball in an empty wheat field. If a home run was hit into the woods at the edge of the field, the game was stopped. During this delay the players looked for the baseball. Jim often caused these game delays, and he joined in the search for the ball—but only after running the bases. Jim also served as pitcher in these games because he threw the baseball harder than the other players.

A Chance to Succeed

On May 12, 1904, Major Mercer, from the Carlisle Indian School in Pennsylvania, visited the Garden Grove school. Mercer came at the request of Jim's father, who had written to him. "I want him to go make something of himself," Hiram wrote, "for he cannot do it here."[1] Several years earlier, at Haskell, Jim had seen the Carlisle football team play. He had wanted to be on such a team, so he decided to attend Carlisle.[2] Thorpe entered the school in June 1904. Nearly sixteen years old, he was not a big youth. He was just five feet five inches, and weighed only 115 pounds.

❖ Thorpe Attends Carlisle ❖

The Carlisle school had been opened on November 1, 1879, by Richard H. Pratt. Pratt was a United States Army officer who formerly led the Tenth Cavalry, which was made up of African-American troopers called Buffalo Soldiers. Pratt's experience with African-American soldiers and Native American scouts made him see that all people are created equal.[3] So Pratt decided to start a school that would give Native Americans a chance to succeed in a white people's world.[4]

The Carlisle school taught trades such as tailoring, carpentry, baking, farming, and stenography to Native Americans. Native American women also attended the school. They learned domestic skills such as sewing and cooking. In addition, the school offered some business courses. Many Carlisle graduates went on to careers in business and law.

Like other Native American schools, Carlisle mainly taught white people's customs to students. Traditional Native American long hair was cut, and only Christian names were used.[5] Like Haskell, the Carlisle school was run in a military style.

Thorpe had wanted to be an electrician, but the school had no courses for this trade. So he began to learn tailoring. Thorpe also played football, in the guard position, for the tailor-shop intramural team.

Shortly after entering Carlisle on June 1, 1904, Jim learned that his father had died of blood poisoning. This was the same disease that took the life of Jim's mother. Hiram had gotten the illness while on a hunting trip. In the early 1900s transportation was slow. So Jim was unable to get to Oklahoma in time for his father's funeral. Once again Jim suffered a great loss. Once again he withdrew from people.[6]

One of the features of the Carlisle school was a program known as "outing." It was based on Pratt's belief that to learn white customs Native Americans needed to spend time living with white people.

On June 17, 1904, Thorpe was sent on an outing to live with the A. E. Buckholz family in Somerton, Pennsylvania. School authorities hoped that this assignment would help Thorpe get over his father's death.[7] At the Buckholz residence Thorpe cooked and cleaned for the Quaker family, earning five dollars a month. Then, in March 1905, Thorpe was sent to James L. Cadwallader's farm in Dolington, Pennsylvania. There he worked as a gardener. On his last outing—from September 15, 1905, to April 8, 1907—Thorpe had the position of foreman on Harby Rozarth's farm in Robbinsville, New Jersey. In this job he supervised other Native American workers, and earned eight dollars a month.

About five years before Thorpe first arrived at the Carlisle school, Pratt had realized the value of a winning sports team.[8] Publicity from a successful team would help Pratt get money to run his school. In a bit of irony, the Carlisle football team became Pratt's winning team. The irony stems from the fact that years earlier Pratt had banned football from being played at Carlisle. He thought the sport was too violent.[9]

In fact, at one point there was such a national outcry for abolishing the game of football, due to its violence, that President Theodore Roosevelt decided to get involved. He called on representatives from Yale, Harvard, and Princeton to meet him at the White House. The president asked the men to rescue the game of football by getting rid of its violent features. "Brutality and foul play," he declared, "should receive the same summary punishment given to a man who cheats at cards."[10]

Eventually, a Football Rules Committee was formed from a conference attended by representatives of sixty-two American colleges. This committee met with the former rules group headed by Walter Camp, an acknowledged football expert. The two merged to form the American Intercollegiate Football Rules Committee, which banned many of the game's dangerous features.

❖ Football Comes to Carlisle ❖

After being petitioned by Carlisle athletes who wanted to play football, Pratt agreed to reinstate the game. His conditions to the athletes were that they play fair and that they eventually sharpen their skills to the point that they could beat the biggest football team in the country.[11] Then, in 1899, Pratt hired Glenn Scobey Warner as Carlisle coach. Warner, who had been a star guard for Cornell University from 1891 to 1894, was known as "Pop." He got this nickname because—at age twenty-five—he was the oldest member on Cornell's football team. He was also the team's captain.

❖ "Pop" Warner Coaches Carlisle ❖

"Pop" Warner, after briefly practicing law, started his coaching career at the University of Georgia in 1895. But it was at Carlisle, starting in 1899, that he gained national fame.

Warner was one of the first coaches to use the forward pass. He taught his quarterbacks to throw the football in a perfect spinning spiral. Warner also used wood and cloth to build the first blocking sleds.

Warner's football teams often relied on speed and deception in order to beat opponents from larger institutions—such as Harvard, University of Pennsylvania, Yale, Syracuse, Princeton, and Army.[12] During that time period, these schools had student enrollments numbering four to five thousand, in comparison to Carlisle's enrollment of one thousand students.

Although Carlisle had fewer athletes to choose from in fielding a football team than other schools, a higher percentage of its players are still ranked among the all-time stars of football.[13] These players include Jim Thorpe, Bemus Pierce, Frank Hudson, Jimmie Johnson, Frank Mount Pleasant, Albert Exendine, Lone Star, and Pete Hauser.

Sometimes Warner used inventive tricks to help his team win or, at least, score points. One such ploy was known as the "hidden ball" trick. Warner used this play in an October 31, 1903, game between Carlisle and Harvard. He had earlier used this play against Penn State, but since the game was not very important, the press did not pick up on the ploy. Warner defended his deception, "I also used the trick at Carlisle to add interest to the scrimmage practice, but we never considered it a strictly legitimate play and only employed it against Harvard as a good joke on the haughty Crimson players."[14]

After a Harvard kickoff, Carlisle quarterback Jimmie Johnson caught the ball on the 5-yard line. The rest of the Carlisle players, facing outward, formed a wedge around Johnson. Johnson quickly stuffed the football under the back of guard Charlie Dillon's jersey. Dillon was six feet tall and could run 100 yards in ten seconds. Then all of the Carlisle players scattered, with the halfbacks tucking their helmets to their chests so that they appeared to be carrying a football. The Harvard defense could not tell which player had the ball. Dillon, running with his hands free, was not even given a second look by the defense.

The fans yelled, seeing the big lump on Dillon's back, but the Harvard team remained confused until Dillon crossed the goal line for the touchdown.[15] Since Warner had told a referee that he might use the hidden ball play, the official ruled that the touchdown was legal and the score would count. Eventually this football play was ruled illegal. In the end, the "hunchback" play did not help Carlisle win; Harvard still defeated the team, 12-11.

In 1915 Warner became coach of the University of Pittsburgh football team. During the next nine years he produced three undefeated teams. Warner moved to Stanford University in 1924. There, he coached three Rose Bowl teams in nine years. Warner's coaching career extended forty-four years, from 1895 to 1939. In 1951, among numerous other honors, Warner was voted the "Coach of All the Years" award. This award was given to retired coaches for notable contributions to football. Warner remains one of the most influential coaches in American collegiate football history. While at Carlisle, Warner gave Pratt the winning team he desired.

❖Thorpe Turns to Track and Field❖

Jim Thorpe returned to Carlisle from his last outing in 1907. He was five feet ten inches, and weighed 144 pounds. One day Thorpe saw several members of the Carlisle track and field team trying to jump a bar set at five feet nine inches. None of them were having any success. They were knocking down the bar with each try. Thorpe asked if he could try to clear the bar. The team members checked out Thorpe's overalls and heavy shoes, and snickered.[16] But they stood back to let Thorpe try. They watched as Thorpe cleared the bar without knocking it down.

When "Pop" Warner—who coached track and field as well as football at Carlisle—heard about Thorpe's feat, he called the young man to his office. Thorpe described the meeting with these words:

> *"Do you know what you have done?" "Pop" asked. "Nothing bad, I hope" was my reply. "Bad" growled the coach. "Boy, you've just broken the school record! That bar was set at five feet nine inches!" "I told 'Pop' I didn't think that [was] very high, that I thought I could do better in a track suit. 'Pop' told me to go down to the clubhouse and exchange those overalls for a track outfit. I was on the track team now."[17]*

Thorpe performed very well in his first track meet. He won the 120-yard hurdles and the high jump. He also finished second in the 220-yard dash. Warner asked Albert Exendine, a Carlisle track and football star, to help train Thorpe. The two athletes

Thorpe, shown here hurling the javelin in a collegiate track and field meet, used Carlisle's 1912 season to prepare for the Olympic games.

— ◈ —

Coach "Pop" Warner (right) asked track star Albert Exendine (left) to help train Thorpe in the finer points of track and field.

became great friends, even when Thorpe broke all Exendine's track and field records by the end of the 1907 season.[18]

Native American athletes often receive the respect from their people that warriors once held. Athletes brought prestige and fame to their people.[19] This situation was true in Thorpe's days. Sports also brought out good qualities in Thorpe. As an athlete, he began to show leadership skills.[20]

During the summer of 1907, Thorpe did not have to go on an outing. He remained at Carlisle to train.

Collegiate Athlete

In September 1907, Thorpe tried out for the Carlisle football team. Coach Warner did not want Thorpe to play football. He did not want his new track star to get injured.[1] But Thorpe really wanted to play the game. Wearing a uniform that was too large, he pestered Warner to let him play. Finally, the tired coach gave in. He pointed to the varsity team on the field. "Give them some tackling practice," he told Thorpe.[2]

On the first play Thorpe took the ball and ran down the field. He left his would-be tacklers clutching the ground. Warner yelled, "You're supposed to give the first team tackling practice, not run through them!"[3] Thorpe quickly responded, "Nobody tackles Jim."[4] Warner let Thorpe run the ball again, and again the quick athlete dodged the defense. Warner decided to let Thorpe on the team. "Get him a uniform that fits," he said.[5]

Later, in 1928, Warner evaluated Thorpe's football talent for the *Christy Walsh Syndicate*. He wrote:

> *He [Thorpe] had speed as well as strength. He knew how to use his strength and speed better than any football player or track athlete I have ever known. He was a great competitive athlete and always did much better in actual competition than he did in practice.*[6]

The 1907 Carlisle football team lost only one game during its season, compiling a 10-1 record and outscoring its opponents 267 to 62. Quarterbacked by Frank Mount Pleasant, the team was becoming a national powerhouse. Thorpe, in line behind talented football players, did not get much playing time. He also needed some time to learn the intricacies of offensive and defensive play. Thorpe's first varsity action was against Syracuse on October 12, 1907; his first varsity start was against Princeton. Throughout the season Thorpe played well, showing promise, but he was not yet a star player.[7]

❖The High Jumpers' Challenge❖

At the start of the 1908 track season, Warner made a challenge to the high jumpers on his team. Any one of them who could jump the bar at five feet ten and a half inches could go to the Penn Relays in Philadelphia, Pennsylvania. Thorpe accepted the challenge and met it, jumping five feet eleven inches.

At the Penn Relays, Thorpe improved on this mark. In Philadelphia he jumped six feet one inch. This mark tied another track and field entrant from Indiana. A coin toss was used to decide the winner. Thorpe won the toss and gained a gold medal.

In a track and field meet against Syracuse, Thorpe placed first in five events—the high and low hurdles, the high and long jumps, and the shot put. Thorpe also placed second in the hammer throw. Next, at the Pennsylvania Intercollegiate Meet in Harrisburg, Thorpe won every event that he entered! He participated in the hammer throw, the high and low hurdles, and the high and long jumps. The new track star broke many records, but this was not what he cared about most. What Thorpe cared about most was winning. Albert Exendine said, "He didn't care about records as such. He badly wanted to win. That was enough."[8]

❖ Thorpe Returns to Football in 1908 ❖

During the 1908 football season, Thorpe's talent began to emerge. It was his first season as a full-time halfback. In Carlisle's first game, against Conway Hall, Thorpe scored five times and passed for another in the first half alone. Carlisle beat the preparatory school, 53-0. Lebanon Valley College, the next opponent, was also shut out, 35-0. Against Villanova, Thorpe's seventy-yard touchdown run in the third quarter won the game for Carlisle.

On October 3, the Carlisle football team played the Penn State Nittany Lions in Wilkes-Barre, Pennsylvania. In this game, Thorpe displayed his kicking ability. He booted three field goals, each worth four points, giving Carlisle a 12-5 victory. Thorpe again exhibited his kicking skill against Syracuse. Only this time Carlisle did not allow its opponents to score. The Orangemen fell, 12-0.

The 1908 Carlisle team had some setbacks as well. It suffered a 17-0 loss at the hands of Harvard and then an 11-6 loss to Minnesota. In a game against the University of Pennsylvania, Thorpe missed several field goals. At the end of the contest, he did break away for a long run, throwing himself across the goal line for a score. The two teams played to a 6-6 tie. Thorpe would call this the toughest game of his life.[9]

Overall, Thorpe's superior athletic skills helped Carlisle win, and win big. The team ended its season with a 10-2-1 record and with the offense outscoring opposing teams, 212 to 55. For his athletic contribution, Thorpe was selected a third-team All-American by Walter Camp.

Camp was recognized as the country's leading football authority at that time. A former halfback at Yale as well as the father of American football, Camp was a member of every rules convention or committee from 1879 until his death. Due to such a prestigious background, Camp's selections of All-America players have been the most commanding ones to football fans.[10]

During the winter months that followed, Thorpe played some basketball on Carlisle's team. He also competed in a few indoor track and field meets. Then it was time for Carlisle's 1909 track and field season.

❖ 1909 Track and Field ❖

In a meet against Lafayette, which was undefeated before competing against Carlisle, Thorpe had an outstanding day in his collegiate track and field career. A popular story tells how Thorpe defeated the forty-eight-member Lafayette team by himself.[11] In fact, he had six other teammates—including Louis Tewanima, a Hopi long-distance runner and future Olympian—to help. But Thorpe's performance, earning more than half of his team's points, was legendary. He won five gold medals—in the 120-yard hurdles, long jump, high jump, shot put, and discus throw. He also won a bronze medal in the 100-yard dash. Carlisle won the meet, 71-41.

That year Thorpe starred in every track and field meet that he entered. He earned at least two gold medals in each of the following: the Georgetown University Athletic Association Meet, the Johns Hopkins University Meet, and the Harrisburg Track Athletic Committee Meet. Thorpe finished the 1909 season by repeating his 1908 performance against Syracuse. He won five gold medals in the same five events as the previous year.

❖ Minor-League Baseball ❖

During the summer of 1909, Thorpe went to North Carolina to play minor-league baseball. He traveled with two Carlisle teammates, Possum Powell and Jesse Young Deer. Thorpe was offered $15 to play third base for the Rocky Mount team. Soon he was also pitching, although Thorpe won only nine out of nineteen games.

❖ Thorpe Heads Home to Oklahoma ❖

In the fall, instead of returning to Carlisle, Thorpe headed home to Oklahoma. He said he was tired of school bells and classwork.[12] Thorpe spent the year helping his sister on her farm. He hunted, fished, and did whatever he pleased.[13]

During the summer of 1910, Thorpe returned to play baseball in the East Carolina Association. That season he played for Fayetteville, North Carolina, under team manager Charley Clancy. But the baseball association had money problems and was unable to pay its players. The league soon folded, and Thorpe returned home to Oklahoma.

❖ **Return to Carlisle and Football** ❖

Two years had passed since Thorpe left Carlisle. One day he met Albert Exendine, who was in Oklahoma. Exendine persuaded Thorpe to return to Carlisle. Thorpe, now twenty-three years old, agreed. Thrilled at the idea of Thorpe's return to football, Coach Warner talked to the school officials at Carlisle.[14] They agreed to let Thorpe return to school.

During the 1911 football season, Carlisle faced teams such as Georgetown, Pittsburgh, Lafayette, Pennsylvania, Harvard, Syracuse, and Brown. These teams included a total of twenty-one All-Americans. Thorpe would be a key weapon when playing such strong opponents.

Upon returning to Carlisle, Thorpe stood about six feet tall and weighed 185 pounds. The two-year layoff from the game did not hurt his football skills. Thorpe's punts were so high and long that he could often get down the field as they were landing. He was an excellent halfback who exhibited both speed and strength. These traits enabled him to run around or through tacklers. Thorpe was a tough defensive player who delivered jarring hits to his opponents.[15]

During the next two years, 1911 and 1912, Thorpe played two of his most memorable football games.[16] One was against Harvard, on November 11, 1911, his first year back at Carlisle. The other was against Army in 1912. Thorpe's performance in these games helped to make him a football legend.

Against the first two opponents of the 1911 season—Lebanon Valley and Muhlenberg—Carlisle won easily. In a Carlisle victory over nearby Dickinson, Thorpe completed an 85-yard run to win the game. Warner's team next overran Mount St. Mary, 46-5. Then the Carlisle team faced Georgetown. Although Thorpe did not score any touchdowns in this game, his running set up his teammates' touchdowns and his kicking added field goal points. Carlisle won the contest, 28-5.

The next team to fall to Carlisle was the University of Pittsburgh. The Carlisle defense did not allow Pittsburgh to score, while the offense racked up 17 points. During the Pittsburgh game Thorpe's punts went 50 to 70 yards, enabling him to run downfield to make the tackle or get the ball himself. Once he received his own punt and ran the 20 yards that were left to make a touchdown.

Against Lafayette, Thorpe scored one touchdown, set up two others, and kicked a 35-yard field goal. He also injured his ankle during that 19-0 victory. Consequently, Thorpe—though present and dressed in uniform—was forced to sit out the next game against Pennsylvania. But the Carlisle team managed a 16-0 win without Thorpe.

— ◈ —

Thorpe's punts were so high and long that he could often get down the field as they were landing.

Throughout the season, stories of Thorpe's football feats were often exaggerated. Many people seemed willing to believe fantastic stories when they involved the great Jim Thorpe. But there was one game during Carlisle's 1911 football season in which Thorpe did excel while not in top physical shape. In a game against the Crimson of Harvard, Thorpe's field goal kicks enabled Carlisle to defeat the previous year's national football champions. He played the game "with his leg swathed in bandages."[17]

Though Thorpe's sprained ankle from two weeks before was not fully healed, he dressed for the game against Harvard. Unlike the Pennsylvania game, however, Thorpe did play in this contest—leading Carlisle to a memorable upset victory. The football game was held at Harvard's stadium before a crowd of more than twenty-five thousand fans. Thorpe carried the ball on three out of every five plays, gaining a total of 173 yards. He also kicked a field goal in every quarter of the game. The field goals were kicked from 13, 43, 37, and 48 yards away. *The New York Times* reported: "All of the kicks were straight between the posts except the last [which still counted for a score], and all of them would have scored had the kicker been 15 or 20 yards further away from the objective point."[18]

For the first three quarters of the game, the Crimson used its second team, and Harvard left the field at halftime with a 9-6 lead. Harvard's first touchdown was scored in the second quarter after Thorpe fumbled at the 45-yard line. A Harvard defensiveman picked up the ball and ran just 5 yards before Thorpe, who had quickly recovered from his mistake, tackled him. Several plays later, Harvard scored on a touchdown run. In the third quarter Carlisle mounted an attack from its 40-yard line that resulted in a touchdown nine plays later. On another series of plays Carlisle got to within 25 yards of the goal line, where Thorpe kicked his third field goal. Harvard was now losing the game.

In the fourth quarter the Crimson's first team was sent onto the field. However, Carlisle moved the ball as well against the first team as it did against the second.[19] Thorpe's final field goal won the game for Carlisle. Harvard was able to score one more touchdown but could not come up with three more points to tie Carlisle. The 18-15 upset of Harvard by Carlisle remains one of the greatest in college football history.[20]

Harvard's Coach Percy Haughton was very impressed with Thorpe that day. He said, "Watching him turn the ends, slash off, tackle, kick, and pass, . . . I realized that here was the theoretical superplayer in flesh and blood."[21]

The following week, after the upset of Harvard, Carlisle lost to Syracuse by one point, 12-11. Thorpe scored two touchdowns in this game, although the points did not help his team win. Returning to its old form, Warner's team beat its last two opponents,

Johns Hopkins and Brown. In the Johns Hopkins game, Thorpe only played in the first two series of downs, but that is all he needed to score twice. Against Brown, he set a record-breaking punt of 83 yards.

The Carlisle football team finished its 1911 season with an 11-1 record. The players elected Thorpe captain for the 1912 season, and Walter Camp selected Thorpe as a first-team All-America halfback. Jim Thorpe was now gaining national attention, with several football experts calling him one of the greatest halfbacks ever to play the game of football.

The *Pittsburgh Dispatch* reported: "This person Thorpe was a host in himself. Tall and sinewy [strong], as quick as a flash and as powerful as a turbine engine, he appeared to be impervious [immune] to injury."[22] Rumors were passed that one college coach guaranteed a varsity letter to whomever broke Thorpe's arm or leg. For good reason, there were no takers.[23]

◆ Thorpe Meets Iva Miller ◆

During this time Iva Miller entered Thorpe's life. Iva was a pretty and popular honor student at the Carlisle school. Thorpe soon fell in love with her.[24] Though Miller attended the Carlisle school, she was not Native American. She became a student at Carlisle when her sister, Grace Miller, a teacher at the school, falsified her enrollment. Grace did this in order to take care of Iva after becoming Iva's guardian after their parents died.[25]

With the passage of winter, the Carlisle's 1912 track and field season soon began. Thorpe used the season's workouts and meets to prepare himself for the upcoming Olympic games. He and teammate Louis Tewanima hoped to win gold medals.[26]

Olympic Athlete

The original Olympic games were played in ancient Greece. In 1896, Baron Pierre de Coubertin of France revived the concept, starting the modern Olympic games, for political purposes. He, as well as the International Olympic Committee (IOC) presidents who succeeded him, wanted to promote better understanding and good feelings among warring nations.[1]

With that purpose in mind, Coubertin designed the Olympic symbol, five colorful rings connected to each other, to represent the five continents and the colors of their various national flags. The procession of athletes from participating countries, beginning with the Greek team and ending with the hosting country's team, is also carried out to symbolize international cooperation.[2]

Athletes participating in the Greek Olympic games were offered support while they trained. However, organizers of the modern games decided that only amateur athletes, those who did not receive material gain for their play or training, could compete. Coubertin supported this ruling.

◈ The Olympics: Amateurs Only ◈

The concept of amateurism was actually created by the Victorian middle and upper classes. Its purpose, which was quite open during that time period, was to exclude the lower class from competing with the upper class. Originally, the amateur rule excluded those who performed any kind of manual labor. Though quite clear, this ruling soon was too obviously undemocratic to be defended.[3] So the ruling was changed to prohibit anyone who received material benefit, directly or indirectly, from playing a sport. Not until the 1990s would professional athletes be allowed to again compete in Olympic games.

Any athlete who earned money by playing a sport was barred from competing in the Olympic games. If an Olympian was found to have received money for playing a sport before he or she won the medals, that athlete would have to return all medals. Also, any records set by that athlete would be removed from the Olympic recordkeeping books.

From 1896 to 1908 the United States Olympic team was made up of rich young athletes from elite sports clubs. Wealthy athletes could afford to play and train without earning money. In 1912, for the first time, open tryouts were held for selection of United States Olympic athletes. Any American citizen could try out for the Olympics at one of several regional sites.

❖ Women Enter Olympic Competition ❖

Also for the first time, in 1912, women were allowed to compete in Olympic swimming and diving events. This ruling increased the number of female athletes from thirty-six in 1908 to fifty-seven in 1912, although this number is in comparison to 2,447 male athletes. However, due to Commissioner Sullivan's opposition to women's sports in general, no American women swam or dove at the Olympics games in Stockholm.[4] The 1912 United States Olympic team was made up of athletes from different ethnic backgrounds. The American team included African-American Howard Porter Drew, Hawaiian Duke Kahanomaku, and Native Americans Jim Thorpe and Lewis Tewanima.

Thorpe tried out for the 1912 United States Olympic team at the Polo Grounds in New York City. He was in top physical shape.[5] At the conclusion of the tryouts, he qualified for both the pentathlon and decathlon Olympic events.

The American Olympic Committee commissioned the USS *Finland* to transport the United States team to Stockholm, Sweden. The steamer included a track, pool, mats, and various other equipment that the Olympic athletes could use to stay in top physical condition. It also had one dining cabin that was set aside for the Olympic competitors.

◈ Traveling to the Olympics ◈

On Friday morning, June 14, 1912, the *Finland*— decorated in the national colors of red, white, and blue—stood ready to depart from its New York pier. On hand for the send-off were five thousand well-wishers, loudly cheering and frantically waving American flags.[6] Then at 9 A.M. the *Finland*, carrying the American Olympians, set off for Europe. This ocean voyage was Thorpe's first, and he really enjoyed it.[7]

Stories that Thorpe did not train during the long trip have been repeated again and again.[8] In fact, Thorpe trained for hours every day. He and Tewanima ran on the special cork track that circled the ship's swimming pool.[9] The cork material was used to help muffle the runners' pounding feet.

Tewanima won a silver medal at the 1912 Olympics. He finished behind a Finnish runner named Johan "Hannes" Kolehmainen in the 10,000-meter long distance race. Fifteen racers qualified for this race, but only eleven started. Then the heat and pace cut the field to just five finishers. Kolehmainen placed first with a time of 31:20.8; while Tewanima, clocked at 32:06.6, placed second.

Years later, Olympic teammate Ralph Craig, a gold-medal winner in both the 100-meter and 200-meter dashes, recalled how Thorpe trained while aboard the *Finland*. He said, "I can certainly remember running laps and doing calisthenics with Jim every day on the ship."[10]

The *Finland* reached Antwerp, Belgium, on Monday, June 24. The United States Olympic team worked out at the Beershot Athletic Club. Then, two days later, the athletes continued their trip to Sweden. The American team arrived in Stockholm on June 29. In these early years of the modern games, there was no Olympic village. So the American team stayed aboard the ship during its time in Sweden. After the opening ceremonies on July 6, the Olympic athletes began competing in their individual events.

Winning an Olympic gold medal in either the pentathlon *or* the decathlon is an impressive achievement. Thorpe's athletic performance earned him Olympic gold medals in *both*. His scores in both events outclassed his rivals "by an incredible margin, which was only broken 30 years later."[11] At the time, the young Native American was humble about his remarkable feats, but he did have confidence in himself. Thorpe said, "I had trained well and hard and had confidence in my ability."[12]

— ◈ —

Thorpe trained on the USS Finland *en route to the 1912 Olympic games in Stockholm, Sweden.*

The American Olympic team won a total of sixteen gold medals, of which two were Thorpe's. In addition to the gold medals, Gustav V presented Thorpe with a bronze bust in the king's likeness. He also gave Thorpe a jeweled silver cup shaped like a Viking ship. This was a gift from Russia's Czar Nicholas II.

Thorpe was now known throughout the world as a great all-around athlete. No other sports figure had ever captured the public imagination so quickly or completely.[13] Before returning home, Thorpe competed in three European track and field exhibitions.

❖ Thorpe Returns to the United States ❖

Once back in the United States, the Olympian received many tributes. First he, Tewanima, and Coach Warner were honored with a parade in Carlisle. Then these three joined the rest of the United States Olympic team in New York for a ticker-tape parade. The procession began at 41st Street and Fifth Avenue and continued to the City Hall in lower Manhattan.

A reporter for *The New York Times* wrote, "Seldom, if ever, has such a demonstration been given to American athletes."[14] All along the parade route crowds of people, including school children, cheered the Olympic athletes. The *Times* reporter further observed, "Thorpe . . . seldom looked to right or left, and rarely ever permitted himself to depart

In the 1912 Olympic decathlon event, Thorpe threw the shot put 12.89 meters (42.28 feet).

from his accustomed stoicism [unresponsiveness]."[15] In addition, Thorpe was honored at a banquet in Philadelphia, Pennsylvania, and he received a letter of congratulations from President William H. Taft.

Thorpe entered the Amateur Athletic Union (AAU) All-Around Championship in Queens, New York. The ten-event track competition was held in just one day. Despite bad weather and a being ill from food poisoning, Thorpe won this championship. His 7,476 point total broke Martin Sheridan's previous record of 7,385 points.

Sheridan was quick to congratulate Thorpe. In speaking to a newspaper reporter he said, "Thorpe is the greatest athlete that ever lived. He has me beaten fifty ways. Even when I was in my prime I could not do what he did today."[16]

◈ Return to Carlisle and Football ◈

As a famous athlete, Thorpe had many offers to play baseball or become an actor. But Coach Warner convinced Thorpe to return to Carlisle for the 1912 football season. Though famous, Thorpe was a team player. Pete Calac, who played football at Carlisle and professionally, said. "Jim never acted like he was better than any of us, in spite of his great fame. He always tried to be just one of the guys."[17]

In the first two games of the season, against Albright College and Lebanon Valley, Warner let the varsity players rest while he played the second team.

Even without Thorpe and its first-string players, Carlisle still enjoyed easy wins, shutting out both teams.

In the Dickinson game, Thorpe scored Carlisle's first two touchdowns. Then the Carlisle team had to punt from deep within its own territory. The center snapped the ball too high and, though he leaped, Thorpe could not catch it. So he turned and chased the rolling ball, taking hold of it in his own end zone. Thorpe looked up to see several defenders closing in on him. Then he started running, twisting, and evading the Dickinson tacklers. Thorpe scored on this play, covering an amazing 110 yards. The final score was Carlisle—34, Dickinson—0.

Warner again used his second team against Villanova, and Carlisle won by a huge margin, 65-0. In the Jefferson and Washington game that followed, Thorpe had four interceptions. These interceptions, along with his high and long punts kept Carlisle from losing the game. The two teams played to a 0-0 tie. Thorpe continued to star in the next several games against Syracuse, Pittsburgh, Georgetown, Toronto, and Lehigh. He scored three touchdowns in both the Syracuse and Pittsburgh games. In the game against Toronto, he averaged 75 yards a punt. And at Lehigh, after intercepting a pass, Thorpe ran 110 yards for a touchdown. In this game, he also threw a pass that covered 67 yards in the air. Carlisle won the contest against Lehigh, 34-14, with Thorpe scoring 28 of those 34 points. Then came the matchup with Army, in which Thorpe played the second most memorable game of his collegiate career.

After traveling to West Point, New York, Coach Warner motivated his players for their match against Army by reminding them that it was the Cadets' fathers and grandfathers who fought Native Americans in years past.[18] Thorpe apparently took this message to heart, went out on the field, and ran through the West Point line "as if it was an open door."[19] He scored 22 of 27 points for Carlisle, averaging more than 10 yards per carry. According to a *New York Times* account, ". . . at times the game itself was almost forgotten while the spectators gazed on Thorpe, the individual, to wonder at his prowess."[20]

Thorpe's shoulder was injured in the second half of the game, and play was delayed for three minutes while he received medical attention. When Thorpe returned to play, the crowd of three thousand people, mainly Army fans, applauded.

In the third quarter, Thorpe created the most spectacular play of the day, though it did not lead to a touchdown.[21] On this play he received an Army punt on the 45-yard line, about halfway between the two sidelines. The punt was a high one, allowing the Cadet players to get downfield and start to swarm Thorpe:

> *His catch and his start were but one motion. In and out, zigzagging first to one side and then to the other, while a flying Cadet went hurling through space, Thorpe wormed his way through the entire Army team. Every Cadet in the game had his*

chance, and every one of them failed. It was not the usual spectacle of the man with the ball outdistancing his opponents by circling them. It was a dodging game in which Thorpe matched himself against an entire team and proved the master. Lines drawn parallel and fifteen feet apart would include all the ground that Thorpe covered on his triumphant dash through an entire team.[22]

One player for Army that year was Dwight D. Eisenhower, later president of the United States. He and another teammate thought that they could stop Thorpe with a "high-low" tackle. One player would hit Thorpe high in the chest area and the other would tackle Thorpe around the ankles. In later years Eisenhower recounted the result of this plan to his younger brother. "He picked himself up, went back to the huddle. [He] took the ball on the next play and ran for another first down."[23]

This upset game between Carlisle and Army encouraged more exaggerations about Thorpe's football ability. One sportswriter wrote that Thorpe received a kickoff and ran 90 yards for a touchdown, which was called back because of a penalty. Then this writer claimed that on the next play Thorpe caught the kickoff again and ran 95 yards for a score that did count.[24] This account is not true. Thorpe did run 45 yards for a touchdown that was not allowed. But on the next play another of Thorpe's teammates caught the punt. The truth is that Carlisle defeated Army, 27-6. The truth is also that Carlisle relied on the amazing running of left halfback Jim Thorpe.

The following week, Carlisle lost to the University of Pennsylvania. This loss, following an upset victory the week before, was a reminder of the team's 1911 loss to Syracuse after beating Harvard. Like the season before, Carlisle regrouped to win its last two games on the schedule. The team beat Springfield, 30-24, and Brown, 32-0. Carlisle's thirty points in the Springfield game were all scored by Jim Thorpe.

Carlisle's football team compiled a 12-1-1 record that year. The offense totaled 504 points while the defense allowed opponents just 114 points. Thorpe was responsible for 198 of the offensive points, scoring 25 of the total 66 touchdowns. At the time, this was the largest number of points ever recorded by a college football player.[25]

For the second year in a row, Walter Camp named Thorpe a first-team All-American. One football official, who witnessed Thorpe score three touchdowns and two field goals in a snowstorm, summed up the athlete's ability with these words. "I've just officiated at a game in which I've seen the greatest football player ever."[26]

Based on his outstanding collegiate football career, the Football Writers Association of America selected Thorpe to the Early All-Time All-America Team, 1869-1919. Since then, Thorpe has been named on almost every all-time All-America team.[27] The only All-America team that he was not named to was the one that Thorpe himself picked in 1938.[28]

Thorpe spent the Christmas holidays in Oklahoma. Then in January 1913, he returned to Carlisle for what would have been his last term. At this time his future seemed very bright. He had Iva Miller as a steady girl-friend, Olympic gold medals, and all-America college football titles. Then on January 22 an article appeared in the *Worcester Telegram* in Massachusetts. It reported that Thorpe had earned money while playing baseball in the East Carolina Association.

The article had been written by reporter Roy Johnson, who had recently talked to Charley Clancy. Clancy was the manager for the Fayetteville team on which Thorpe had played baseball several years before. Clancy had a picture of Thorpe on his wall. When Johnson questioned how Clancy had this picture of Thorpe, the baseball manager said that Thorpe had played on his Fayetteville team. Clancy did not think about how his words would affect Thorpe.[29]

◈ Amateur Status Questioned ◈

The question of whether or not Thorpe was an amateur athlete while competing in the 1912 Olympics was quickly raised. When the AAU learned of Thorpe's "professional" career, it demanded an explanation from the Olympian. Thorpe admitted that he did earn money while playing baseball. In a letter to AUU Secretary James Sullivan, he wrote: "I did not play for the money there was in it, . . . but because I liked to play ball. I was not wise in the ways of the world and did not realize this was wrong, and that it would make me a professional in track sports."[30]

Other athletes had received money for playing sports, but they played under false names. One such athlete, named "Wilson," was supposedly Dwight D. Eisenhower.[31] The AAU did not accept ignorance of the amateur rule as a valid excuse.[32] The AAU demanded that Thorpe give back his gold medals and other Olympic valuables that he received. The IOC erased Thorpe's name from the record books.

◈ Thorpe's Medals Given Up ◈

Ferdinand Bie, pentathlon runner-up, and Hugo Wieslander, decathlon runner-up, were given Thorpe's gold medals. Some reports indicated that the second-place winners refused to take the medals.[33] This information is also not true. Bie and Wieslander did accept the medals, although they said that if the AAU decision were ever changed, they would return the medals to Thorpe.[34]

Olympic officials thought that by enforcing the amateur rule on Thorpe, other athletes would learn a lesson.[35] But many people supported Thorpe. The amateur rule seemed unfair when not applied to everyone. The AAU's punishment was very difficult for Thorpe to accept.[36]

Thorpe tried to hide his disappointment, but years later the loss of his gold medals still pained him.[37] Thorpe expressed his feelings to John ("Chief") Meyers. Meyers, also a Native American, was

Thorpe's roommate while the two traveled with the New York Giants baseball team. In later years Meyers, a catcher for the Giants, recalled Thorpe's words:

> *I remember, very late one night, Jim came in and woke me up. I remember it like it was only last night. He was crying and tears were rolling down his cheeks. "You know, Chief," he said, "the King of Sweden gave me those trophies, he gave them to me. But they took them away from me. They're mine, Chief, I won them fair and square." It broke his heart and he never really recovered.*[38]

PROFESSIONAL ATHLETE

On February 1, 1913, ten days after the Thorpe "scandal" was first printed, Thorpe signed a contract to play professional baseball with the New York Giants. In accepting this offer, he turned down many other opportunities to get paid for his athletic ability. One promoter offered Thorpe $50,000 to become a professional boxer. Another wanted to pay him $1,000 for performing feats of strength. In addition, owners of several major-league baseball teams wanted Thorpe to play for them. They knew that Thorpe's baseball skill was not the best, but they also knew that his name would sell extra tickets to games.[1]

The New York Giants' manager John "Muggsy" McGraw offered Thorpe $6,000 a year to play for the next three years. Thorpe also received a $5,000 bonus for signing the contract. This was a lot of money for a new player who had no professional experience.[2] After signing the contract with baseball's No. 1 team, Thorpe withdrew from Carlisle. He was twenty-six years old.

◈ Thorpe Plays Professional Baseball ◈

Compared to more experienced baseball players, Thorpe did not play that well.[3] He had an excellent throwing arm, but his fielding and batting statistics were mediocre.[4] McGraw soon sent Thorpe to a

— ◈ —

Jim Thorpe was a professional baseball player with the New York Giants.

minor-league team in Milwaukee, Wisconsin, to work on his baseball skills.

◈ Wedding Bells for Thorpe and Miller ◈

In October 1913 Thorpe married Iva Miller in a wedding ceremony at Carlisle. The two honeymooned in Europe, Egypt, and Japan while Thorpe was on tour with the New York Giants. The major-league team had recently called back Thorpe from Wisconsin so that he could take part in a worldwide exhibition trip with the Chicago White Sox. The couple returned to the United States aboard the *Lusitania* and moved into an apartment near the Polo Grounds. Then Thorpe headed to Marlin Springs, Texas, to attend spring training.

Thorpe started the 1914 baseball season with improved batting skills. He was also a very quick base runner.[5] But McGraw still did not play Thorpe very

— ◈ —

In October 1913, Thorpe married Iva Miller. The ceremony took place in Carlisle, Pennsylvania.

much. In fact, during Thorpe's three years with the Giants, he played only sixty-six games.

The Thorpes' first child, James Jr., was born in 1915. During the next eight years of their marriage, three daughters—Gail, Charlotte, and Grace—were born.

Thorpe spent the entire 1916 baseball season in Milwaukee. At the start of the 1917 season, he was sent to play with Cincinnati.

In 1918 James Jr. died of infantile paralysis. Thorpe would later say that his son's death was the worst time of his life, and that having to give back his gold medals did not even come close to such a terrible feeling.[6]

❖ Thorpe Is Sent to the Minor Leagues ❖

Because McGraw was a strict coach and Thorpe liked to have fun, the two had many run-ins.[7] Their personality conflict came to a head in the 1919 season. During a game, McGraw signaled to Thorpe, who was on base. Thorpe did not see the signal. McGraw called Thorpe a "dumb Indian," which upset Thorpe.[8] Thorpe started to chase McGraw, but Thorpe's teammates stopped him.

Thorpe was soon sent to the Boston Braves, where his major-league baseball career ended with that season. During the next nine years Thorpe played minor-league baseball. He earned batting averages of .327 with Boston in 1919; .360 with Akron in 1920; .358

with Toledo in 1921; and .308, including three home runs in one game with Portland, in 1922. Thorpe played his last official baseball game in 1928 with Akron; he was forty years old.

◈ Thorpe Enters Professional Football ◈

Thorpe played his first professional football game in Canton, Ohio, in 1915. He would play the game during the fall months, returning to baseball in the spring. During this time period, football was not a big-time sport. Teams played in small towns, statistics were not recorded, and players' salaries were not in the millions as they are today.

In 1915 the manager of the Canton Bulldogs, Jack Cusak, talked to Thorpe. The Canton Bulldogs, a professional football team, was located in Ohio. Cusak offered Thorpe $250 per game to play for the Bulldogs.

Cusak's business advisors thought that he was being foolish to pay Thorpe so much money.[9] But Cusak's promotional gamble turned out to be worth it. He later said. "The deal paid off even beyond my greatest expectations. . . . Whereas our paid attendance averaged about 1,200 before we took him [Thorpe] on, we filled the Massillon and Canton parks for the next two games—6,000 for the first and 8,000 for the second."[10]

In baseball, Thorpe was more of a fan attraction than a star player. However, in football, Thorpe was both. Not only did he draw fans; he also helped his team to win. Thorpe became a full-time player for the Canton Bulldogs after the second game of the 1916 season. He started as halfback and also served as head coach. Thorpe's presence increased enthusiasm for the game as well as profits.[11]

Thorpe's first professional football game was in Canton, Ohio, in 1915, against the Massillon Tigers. The Tigers were an Ohio team that included Knute Rockne. Once Rockne tackled Thorpe two times in a row for a loss of yards. The next time Thorpe received the ball, he ran right into Rockne, knocking him unconscious. When Rockne was pulled to his feet, Thorpe slapped him on the shoulder and said, "That's better, Knute. These people want to see Big Jim run!"[12]

In 1915 the Canton Bulldogs, led by Thorpe, beat the Massillon Tigers in the professional football championship game, 4-0. The next year, the Bulldogs and Tigers played to a scoreless tie in the first of two games to decide who would be the football champions. In the second game at Canton, the Bulldogs ran all over the Tigers, winning, 24-0. The teams performed before ten thousand fans—at the time, the largest turnout ever in professional football.[13]

The 1917 professional football season felt the effects of America's involvement in World War I. Teams had difficulty finding players, and game attendance was down. Still, the Bulldogs completed their schedule. The Canton team beat the Massillon Tigers, 14-3, in their first matchup. Then in their second meeting, on December 3, Canton fell to its archrival. The Tigers were able to score two field goals for a 6-0 victory over the Bulldogs.

Thorpe was a football player of great talent. He could run, pass, block, tackle as well as kick. In 1919 he kicked a 95-yard field goal to win a game. Although a wind helped extend the kick's distance, football fans called it the greatest kick ever.[14]

In 1920 representatives of the eleven professional football teams met in Canton, Ohio. These representatives formed the American Professional Football Association (APFA) and elected Jim Thorpe as its president. The league consisted of the following eleven teams: Decatur Staleys, Canton Bulldogs, Akron Professionals, Dayton Triangles, Massillon Tigers, Rock Island Independents, Chicago Cardinals, Hammond Pros, Muncie Tigers, Rochester All-Stars, and the Cleveland Indians. The entry fee for joining this league was set at $100, but no money changed hands.[15] Two years later this organization became the National Football League (NFL). Today the cost of entering a team in this league is millions of dollars.

For six years Thorpe played with the Canton Bulldogs. A strong man, he played hard. According to George Halas, who played for the Hammond Pros against Thorpe, Thorpe's trademark was a defensive body block, delivered at top speed. He said, "Jim never used his arms in orthodox [standard] tackling style. Instead, he hunched his shoulders and rammed his 210 pounds into the ball carrier."[16]

Defensive players needed to be tough when Thorpe broke through the line. He ran with his knees high, and he could only be tackled with a clean, hard hit. Players that tried to tackle Thorpe with just their arms claimed it was like hitting an oak tree.[17]

In one game a lineman from another team kept hitting Thorpe after he was tackled and down on the ground. On the next play, Thorpe took the ball on the handoff. He stopped and placed the football on the ground. When the lineman picked up the ball, Thorpe knocked him out with a bruising tackle. "You must not do that to Jim," he said.[18]

Joe Carr replaced Thorpe as APFA president in 1921. That same year Thorpe switched football teams, signing with Cleveland. In an early game against Cincinnati, however, Thorpe broke his ribs. This injury kept him from playing during the rest of the season.

In 1922 Thorpe joined a football team called the Oorang Indians. The team was started by Walter Lingo, a dog breeder and owner of Oorang Airedale Kennels in La Rue, Ohio, as well as Thorpe's hunting buddy. The players on the team were all Native Americans. Before games started or during halftime, the Oorang players would perform war dances in costume. Airedale exhibitions would also be held. The team played for two seasons, compiling records of 3-6 and 1-10. After the 1923 season, members of the Oorang team went their separate ways.

In 1924, at thirty-six and playing with the Rock Island Independents, Thorpe's athletic ability was beginning to fade.[19] However, his kicking skill was not affected by his age. Sometimes he displayed his punting ability before a game started. He could easily drop kick field goals from the middle of the field.[20]

◆ Thorpe and Kirkpatrick Marry ◆

In 1925 Thorpe was playing football with the New York Giants and the Rock Island Independents. With his athletic career beginning to decline, Thorpe looked to his personal life for fulfillment.[21] In 1923 Iva Miller and Thorpe had divorced. In October 1925 Thorpe married Freeda Kirkpatrick. She was a Scotch-Irish woman from Ohio who was the daughter of a golf-club manager. The couple had four sons—Carl Phillip, William, Richard, and John. Thorpe's children remember him as a man who tried his best to make a living and give them a happy life.[22] In her book *Thorpe's Gold* (written with Brad Steiger), daughter Charlotte Thorpe said, "Young and old loved him [Thorpe] for what he was—a big, warm, fun-loving boy-man."[23]

❖ Thorpe Announces His Retirement ❖

In 1925, at age thirty-seven, Thorpe announced his retirement from sports. He was going to hunt and fish with friends in Yale, Oklahoma. He said, "One must quit sometime. My earning days at sport are at an end and while sports have been my livelihood, I really played for the love of competition."[24]

However, Thorpe still continued to play sports. Coaxed out of retirement, he played occasionally with various teams for several more years. Thorpe played with St. Petersburg in 1926, Canton in 1927, Portsmouth in 1928, and both Hammond and Chicago in 1929. The last time Thorpe wore an official uniform it was that of the Chicago Cardinals. The team lost the game, 34-0. Thorpe, at age forty-one, played his last professional football game.

Jim Thorpe married Freeda Kirkpatrick in October 1925. They had four sons before divorcing in 1941.

LIFE AFTER SPORTS

Career transitions are often difficult, especially for famous athletes. Many athletes miss the attention and the money that they received while playing sports. At first, Thorpe's fame as an athlete helped him find employment. His celebrity status helped him get a job as a referee of dance marathons. Dance marathons were events in which two people competed for cash prizes by dancing as long as they were physically able. Then, in 1929, Thorpe sold the rights to a film about his life story to Metro-Goldwyn-Mayer (MGM). The movie was to be called *The Red Son of Carlisle,* but it was never made by

MGM. The payment that Thorpe received for his life's story was just $1,500.

In 1930, with the Great Depression just beginning, Thorpe agreed to be master of ceremonies for the Bunion Derby. This was an international cross-country marathon race. But the event went bankrupt, and Thorpe had to sue its promoter Charlie C. "Cash and Carry" Pyle, for his pay—a mere $50.

❖ Thorpe Lands Several Movie Roles ❖

Thorpe was next hired as a painter for an oil firm in Los Angeles, California. When this job ended he went to Hollywood and tried out for a small role in a movie. Thorpe was hired to play Chief Black Crow. Later MGM hired Thorpe for a baseball film and a football film that included his former coach "Pop" Warner.

Once, during the filming of a movie, Thorpe took part in a bet among the extras. While waiting for their turn to act, they decided to wager on who could perform the best standing long jump. Most of the extras were young college athletes. Bill Frawley, who later played Fred Mertz on the television show *I Love Lucy*, found out who Thorpe was. So he bet that the "old" man (who was actually an Olympic gold-medal winner) could jump farther than the younger competitors. Thorpe took a few stretches and then took his turn. He leaped 3 meters, 20 centimeters (10 feet, 8 inches). This mark was only 15 centimeters (6 inches) less than the world record at that time.[1] Frawley won the bet.

The Great Depression was becoming more severe, and jobs were becoming harder and harder to find. Thorpe found employment as a laborer; he was hired to help dig the foundation in the building of the Los Angeles County Hospital. For this strenuous work, Thorpe received only fifty cents an hour.

❖ 1932 Olympic Games ❖

Just before the opening of the 1932 Olympics, the press reported that Thorpe could not afford to buy a ticket to the summer games. In fact, many people did not have money to attend the 1932 Olympic games. With just six months until the opening of the games, no national Olympic Committee had responded to the invitations sent out by the American delegation. Budget cuts due to the now worldwide Depression created travel problems for many, including those coming from Europe and South America.[2] In addition, President Herbert Hoover refused to attend.

However, in response to the press reports, people throughout the country offered to get Thorpe a seat at the Olympics.[3] When Vice President Charles Curtis, himself of Native American heritage, heard about Thorpe's situation, he made arrangements for Thorpe to sit with him. Curtis was the person to officially declare the opening of the 1932 Olympic games. He and Thorpe watched track and field star Mildred

"Babe" Didrikson. They also watched a lacrosse exhibition in which a Native American starred. This skilled Mohawk athlete later played the role of Tonto, under the name of Jay Silverheels, in the television program *The Lone Ranger.*[4]

Olympic rules allowed Didrikson to participate in only three events, and she performed well in all three. Didrikson won gold medals in both the 80-meter hurdles and the javelin throw—setting new world records in both—and she took the silver medal in the high jump event. During the Olympic games, Thorpe's presence was announced to the crowd. The people attending the Olympics that day numbered one hundred five thousand. They responded to Thorpe's announced presence by giving him a standing ovation.

In addition to his minor acting roles, Thorpe began to accept offers to speak in public. He did not charge very much money for his appearances, and sometimes he charged no money at all. On December 6, 1934, Thorpe spoke to the students of Poly High School. He ended his talk with: "Athletics give you a fighting spirit to battle your problems of life, and they build sportsmanship."[5]

By the late 1930s, the movie industry began to grow. Consequently, Thorpe began to receive more film work. The size of his parts also increased. He had major roles in the movies *She* and *The Green Light;* he also acted in the film *You Can't Take It With You.*

In 1937 Thorpe returned to Oklahoma to address the situation of his fellow Native Americans. In 1824, the United States government created the Bureau of Indian Affairs (BIA) as a special agency to handle problems involving Native Americans. Along with governing reservations, the BIA was responsible for providing Native Americans with education, employment opportunities, and medical care. The bureau was also charged with helping Native Americans improve their agricultural output through irrigation methods and new farming practices.

Thorpe wanted Native Americans to manage their own lives and property.[6] So, in 1937, he campaigned for Native Americans to abolish the BIA. Thorpe proposed the Wheeler bill, which would allow a group of tribe members to handle Native American issues. The Wheeler bill, however, failed to pass the legislature.

In 1938 Thorpe was hired by MGM to work on the movie *Northwest Passage*. When the filming of this movie was completed, Thorpe returned home to Inglewood, California. He soon found himself named to the all-time All-America football player lists compiled by Knute Rockne, Grantland Rice, and Fielding Harry Yost. Upon the publication of these lists, the press renewed its interest in Thorpe, publishing articles about the famous athlete's accomplishments.[7]

As a result of this publicity, Thorpe was offered a job as a lecturer on a nationwide tour of schools.

Wearing Native American traditional dress, Thorpe spoke to hundreds of students about his athletic career, the value of sports, and something very dear to his heart—Native American people and culture.[8]

Although Thorpe's public speaking engagements earned him money, they kept him on the road. Thorpe traveled thousands of miles through the states of Maryland, Pennsylvania, New York, Massachusetts, Connecticut, and New Jersey. Sometimes he spoke three times in one day. Thorpe was often away from his family for long stretches at a time. On April 4, 1941, after more than fifteen years of marriage, he and his wife Freeda were divorced. This was Thorpe's second marriage to end in divorce.

— ◈ —

An elderly Jim Thorpe is shown here dressed in a Native American costume.

❖World War II Begins❖

When the United States entered World War II in 1941, Thorpe was fifty-three years old. Despite his desire to help his country by enlisting in the military, he was considered too old for active duty.[9] Harry Bennett, who worked for auto manufacturer Henry Ford, heard that Thorpe wanted to help in the war effort. So he offered Thorpe a job on the security staff of Ford's River Rouge Plant in Michigan. The entire staff consisted of athletes from various sports. Thorpe accepted the job and began work on March 20, 1942.

Eleven months after taking the job with Ford, in February 1943, Thorpe suffered a heart attack. He received many letters from concerned fans, including children who, though not old enough to have seen Thorpe play, had heard about his greatness from adults.[10] After being discharged from the hospital, Thorpe returned to Oklahoma to rest and recover. On November 29, 1943, Thorpe resigned from his job with Ford Motor Company. He remained in Oklahoma, staying with friends.

On June 2, 1945, Thorpe married Patricia Gladys Askew—from Louisville, Kentucky—who had been a fan of his since his days as a professional football player. Soon after, Thorpe was accepted into the merchant marine and assigned to the USS *Southwest Victory*. The ship's mission was to carry ammunition to British and American troops in India. In Calcutta, Thorpe spoke to American soldiers.

Thorpe came back to the United States on September 7, 1945. During the next three years, two attempts to have Thorpe's gold medals returned to him met with failure. Meanwhile, Thorpe resumed his lecturing career. Thorpe's third wife, Patricia, a sharp businessperson, helped convince him to charge more for his public addresses—$500 per appearance, plus expenses.

While lecturing, Thorpe often talked about the importance of physical fitness for children—both boys and girls. He considered it a solution to juvenile delinquency. "Sports will improve health and keep the children out of trouble," he told his audiences.[11]

❖ Thorpe Helps Chicago Parks ❖

In March 1948, Thorpe was hired as a staff member of the Chicago Park District's recreation department. His job was to travel throughout Chicago, teaching basic track skills to young people. This assignment enabled him to put into practice his theory of sports. By involving the city's young people in sports, Thorpe was helping them to improve their health and to stay out of trouble. Although Thorpe was living in Chicago, he was still known nationally. As the years passed, more people recognized Thorpe's great contribution to the growth of professional sports. In fact, he received an honor for his contributions shortly after World War II.

At a 1948 football game between the San Francisco 49ers and the Baltimore Colts, Thorpe was honored along with Pop Warner and football star Ernie Nevers. During halftime, the sixty-year-old Thorpe put on a uniform and displayed his kicking ability to the crowd.

After his job in Chicago, Thorpe helped to condition the Israeli National Soccer Team for its match against the United States Olympic Soccer team. The contest was played at New York's Polo Grounds on September 26, 1948. At halftime, comedian Milton

— ❖ —

In 1948, Thorpe was hired as a staff member of the Chicago Park District's recreation department. Here, Thorpe runs with a group of girls during a Junior Olympics event on Chicago's South Side.

Berle joked with the crowd. Then Thorpe displayed his skill at kicking footballs. Twice he punted the ball from midfield—first in one direction and then in the opposite direction. The first kick went 70 yards and the second one went 75 yards. With twenty-five thousand people watching, however, the Israeli team lost to the United States team, 3-1.

❖ Warner Brothers Makes Movie ❖

In August 1949, MGM sold the rights to Thorpe's story to Warner Brothers. Warner cast legendary actor Burt Lancaster to play the role of Thorpe in a film titled *Jim Thorpe—All-American.* Thorpe, who did not make any money from the sale of the movie rights, was employed by Warner as a technical advisor. He helped Lancaster with the basics of kicking a football. A poll of 391 sportswriters and broadcasters voted Thorpe the Greatest Football Player of the Half-Century in January 1950. In this poll by the Associated Press, Thorpe received more votes than such football stars as Harold "Red" Grange, Bronko Nagurski, Ernie Nevers, and Sammy Baugh.

The following month Thorpe was recognized with another honor. He was selected the Best Male Athlete of Half a Century. To win this distinction, Thorpe received a total of 262 votes. The rest of the field combined received only 141 votes.

Competition for the Best Male Athlete of Half a Century award was very strong. Jim Thorpe was

— ❖ —

Thorpe is shown here at age sixty-one kicking a football at New York's Polo Grounds.

compared to many other sports legends including baseball standout Babe Ruth, who finished second, and champion boxer Jack Dempsey, the third-place winner. Thorpe also won more votes than great athletes such as baseball's Ty Cobb, golf's Bobby Jones, football's Red Grange, and track and field's Jesse Owens, who won four gold medals in the 1936 Olympic games. Thorpe's female counterpart to this award was Babe Didrikson Zaharias, whom Thorpe watched during the 1932 Olympics. In addition to winning gold medals in Olympic track events, Babe was a champion professional golfer.

The large number of votes for Thorpe was not meant to diminish the greatness of the other athletes. The votes were meant as tribute to a man who was as close to a superman as any human being could be.[12]

Further recognition of Thorpe's football skill followed in 1950. He was elected to the National College Football Hall of Fame. Shortly thereafter he was elected to the Helms Hall Professional Football Hall of Fame.

In August 1951, Warner's movie about Thorpe's life was finally released. The film opened in two places, Oklahoma City and Carlisle, on August 23. Thorpe traveled to Carlisle for festivities in his honor. He was joined by his son Carl and the actress Phyllis Thaxter who played his first wife in the film. At 5:00 P.M. Thorpe and his entourage attended the unveiling of a marker honoring the athlete. Then a motorcade escorted the group to Dickinson College Gymnasium for an "All-American" banquet that included five hundred guests. After the banquet, the motorcade headed to the Carlisle Theater for the premiere of the Thorpe movie.

Since the late 1940s, many people, including famous athletes, sportswriters, and political figures, tried to have Thorpe's Olympic gold medals returned to him. However, each request was rejected by the IOC, as was this last one. The president of the committee

— ◆ —

During festivities for the premiere of Jim Thorpe—
All-American, *a tablet in Thorpe's honor was unveiled in the
town square. Shown here (left to right) are Sergeant Carl
Thorpe (Thorpe's son), Jim Thorpe, Phyllis Thaxter (the
actress who played Thorpe's first wife in the movie), John S.
Fine (governer of Pennsylvania), and Brigadier General Arthur
Trudeau (commander of the Carlisle Army War College).*

then was Avery Brundage, who happened to have competed in the 1912 Olympics along with Thorpe.

Before those Olympic games began, Brundage was the favorite to win the pentathlon and decathlon. But he did not live up to these expectations. Brundage placed only sixth in the pentathlon, and he never even finished the decathlon.

◆ Thorpe Has Cancer of the Lip ◆

November 1951 found Thorpe in Philadelphia, Pennsylvania. He was leading a Native American singing and dancing group called "The Jim Thorpe Show." While in that city, Thorpe went to the Lankenau Hospital to seek treatment for an infection on his lip. The doctors discovered a cancerous tumor on his lip, and recommended surgery. At the time Thorpe did not have much money to pay for surgery to remove the cancer. So his wife formed the Fair Play for Thorpe Committee to collect donations. Many people responded to Thorpe's need, contributing over $4,500 to the committee. The money helped pay the hospital bills. Thorpe recovered from the cancer on his lip.

Then in September 1952 he suffered his second heart attack at his home in Nevada. Unconscious, he was rushed to the hospital and listed in serious condition. Within three days, however, Thorpe walked out of the hospital.

❖Thorpe Suffers a Fatal Heart Attack❖

Thorpe's third, and fatal, heart attack occurred on March 28, 1953, two months before celebrating his sixty-fifth birthday. It was also the year that Dwight D. Eisenhower, a former collegiate football opponent of Thorpe's, became president of the United States.

Thorpe was eating dinner with his wife, Patricia, at their trailer home, located at the Victory Trailer Court in Lomita, California, when he had his third and final heart attack. Hearing Patricia's screams, a neighbor, Colby Bradshaw, came running. He administered artificial respiration for almost half an hour. Then a county fire rescue squad arrived and revived Thorpe for a few moments. He spoke to the people around him before a relapse hit him. Thorpe could not be revived again.[13] Except for memories, photographs, and record books, a legend was gone.

Jim Thorpe Remembered

Patricia Thorpe made arrangements for a funeral service in Los Angeles, California. At this service more than four hundred relatives and friends recited the Rosary for Thorpe. Then another three thousand mourners filed past his open casket. Thorpe's body was dressed in a tan chamois Indian jacket, and placed in his hands were the Rosary and a Carlisle bible.[1] Numerous tributes and condolences were sent to Patricia, including a telegram from President Eisenhower and a gift of flowers from the Norwegian Sports Association.

Thorpe's body was moved to Oklahoma and temporarily placed in a mausoleum in Shawnee. In the meantime a committee was organized to raise money for a tomb to be built for Thorpe. The Oklahoma state legislature approved $25,000 for the building of a tomb and monument in Shawnee, but in 1954 this measure was vetoed by Governor William Murray. Patricia then had Thorpe's body moved to a mausoleum in Tulsa, Oklahoma.

Patricia made several attempts to find a suitable resting place for her husband, but each met with failure. Then she worked out an agreement with the town of Mauch Chunk, located in northeastern Pennsylvania. This town, which Jim Thorpe had never visited, was experiencing tough economic times due to the decline of the coal industry. The townspeople had created a fund—collecting a nickel a week—to bring new industry into their area of the Lehigh Valley. After some discussion, Patricia said she would move Thorpe's body to Mauch Chunk, provided the town would change its name to Jim Thorpe. Residents voted and agreed to consolidate the two small towns of Mauch Chunk and East Mauch Chunk, naming the unified town Jim Thorpe. The high school also changed its name to Jim Thorpe.

Patricia signed an agreement with the town borough, and Thorpe's body was moved from Oklahoma to Pennsylvania. Until a monument could be built, Thorpe's body was placed in a temporary crypt in the

Evergreen Cemetery. Two years went by and the National Fraternal Order of Eagles did not come through with the money to build a monument to Thorpe as promised. So the town of Jim Thorpe made arrangements with the Summit Hill Marble and Granite Company to help it build the $10,000 mausoleum. The town used money from its nickel-a-week-fund to construct the mausoleum. To help save the town money, volunteers did all the labor at the site of the mausoleum.

The mausoleum of Minnesota red granite was dedicated on May 31, 1957. Over five thousand people—including Thorpe's widow, three daughters, three grandchildren, friends, and teammates—attended the ceremony. One highlight of the two-hour dedication was the distribution of earth around the mausoleum.[2] Soil from areas that were important in Thorpe's life and athletic career was scattered at the site. Mrs. Sadie Feder, a Native American princess from Oklahoma City, spread soil taken from Thorpe's birthplace in Prague, Oklahoma. John (Hans) Lobert, Thorpe's teammate during his years with the New York Giants baseball team, spread soil from the Polo Grounds. Then Pete Calac, Thorpe's one-time Carlisle teammate, spread soil from the Olympic Stadium in Stockholm, Sweden. Soil from the field at the Carlisle Indian School was also distributed at the site.

— ❖ —

On May 31, 1957, Thorpe's mausoleum in Jim Thorpe, Pennsylvania, was dedicated.

The front of the mausoleum is inscribed with King Gustav's words: "Sir, you are the greatest athlete in the world." Also inscribed on the front of the mausoleum are Thorpe's name and the dates of his birth (1888) and death (1953). The four sides of the mausoleum are decorated with carvings of Thorpe engaged in the sports of football, baseball, and track and field. The carvings also include one that depicts Thorpe's heritage. It shows Thorpe astride a horse dressed in Native American clothing, including headdress. The memorial is a quiet, dignified place located in a small field along Route 903, just beyond the main business district in the town of Jim Thorpe. The site of the mausoleum has sprouted no souvenir stores or restaurants.

Since his death, Thorpe has received numerous honors and tributes. In 1955 the NFL named its annual most valuable player award the Jim Thorpe Trophy. Also each year a Jim Thorpe award is given to the best collegiate defensive back.

In addition to being voted into the National College Football Hall of Fame, Thorpe has been elected to several others. He was elected to the National Indian Hall of Fame in 1958, the Pennsylvania Hall of Fame in 1961, the National Football Hall of Fame in 1963, and the National Track and Field Hall of Fame in 1975.

❖Jim Thorpe Day is Celebrated❖

In 1967 "Jim Thorpe Day" was held in Yale, Oklahoma. At that time the Oklahoma Historical Society in Yale was made "The Home of Jim Thorpe." Thorpe's portrait, painted by Charles Banks Wilson, was hung in the rotunda of Oklahoma's state capitol in Oklahoma City. Thorpe's home in Yale, Oklahoma—where he lived with Iva Miller—was later purchased by the state and opened to the public for visitation.

"Project Jim Thorpe Day" was created by the Carlisle Jaycees and Pennsylvania Governor Raymond P. Shafer. Over five thousand signatures were collected from people who wanted Thorpe's gold medals returned and his records reinstated. The petition was sent to the United States Olympic Committee.

In 1973 the AAU restored Thorpe's amateur status during the 1909-1912 period. This decision helped get back Thorpe's Olympic gold medals. In 1982 the IOC voted to reinstate Thorpe's Olympic records and return his medals. The driving forces behind the IOC's reversal regarding Thorpe were Robert Wheeler, a biographer of Thorpe, and his wife Florence Ridlon. In 1982 the two created the Jim Thorpe Foundation, which was dedicated to returning Thorpe's Olympic medals as well as educating people about Thorpe's athletic accomplishments.

During research of the 1912 Olympic bylaws, Florence Ridlon learned that protests regarding the qualifications of an Olympic competitor had to be made in writing and received by the Olympic Committee within thirty days of the distribution of the medals. The newspaper report that caused Thorpe's amateur status to be revoked was not published until almost seven months after the completion of the 1912 Olympic games.

For seventy years Olympic officials said that ignorance was no excuse for Thorpe's breaking of the amateur rules. Now, Wheeler and Ridlon used these words against the officials. They told the IOC, "Gentlemen, with all due respect, ignorance of the general regulations for the 1912 Olympics was no excuse for illegally divesting [stripping] Jim Thorpe of his awards."[3] With that argument in place, the IOC reversed the seventy-year position it had taken in the Thorpe case.

Jim Thorpe would now be recognized as the Olympic champion he had always been. However, in the record books, Thorpe is listed as "co-winner" with Ferdinand Bie in the pentathlon and Hugo Wieslander in the decathlon.

❖ Thorpe's Medals are Returned ❖

The IOC issued duplicate gold medals that were presented to six of Thorpe's seven children on January 18, 1983, at an IOC meeting. Thorpe's son John, who at the time was chief of the Sac and Fox tribe, attended in official tribal dress. Silver replicas of the

Olympic medals were also given to Thorpe's children. In addition to Thorpe's children, most of Thorpe's thirteen grandchildren and sixteen great grandchildren attended the presentation. The bronze bust of Gustav V and the silver cup were never returned to Thorpe's family, although they were displayed at the 1984 Olympics. Thorpe's daughter Charlotte called the campaign to return her father's Olympic medals the "70-year marathon."[4]

In 1984, forty male and female runners participated in the relay of the Olympic torch. The runners began at the Onondaga Reservation near Syracuse, New York, and ended in Los Angeles, California—site of the Summer Olympics that year. The three thousand six hundred mile trek took two months and was called "The Great Jim Thorpe Longest Run." A grandson of Jim Thorpe, Bill Jr., helped carry the torch in this relay. Among other runners he was also joined by Gina Hemphill, granddaughter of Jesse Owens, winner of four track-and-field gold medals at the 1936 Summer Olympics in Berlin, Germany.

Thorpe's extraordinary athletic ability continues to be recognized in the sports world. During the 1996 Summer Olympics, the Olympic torch relay route—from Los Angeles, California, to Atlanta, Georgia—was changed to include Prague, Oklahoma, Thorpe's birthplace. Originally the Atlanta Committee for the Olympic Games had the torch relay running through Yale, Oklahoma. The committee mistakenly thought this town was Thorpe's birthplace. After much discussion and apologies, the committee agreed to reroute the relay through Prague rather than Yale. Sam Muzny of the Prague Historical Society had this to say about the brief controversy: "It's like the Olympic people can never get it right. They took his medals away. Now they get his birthplace wrong."[5]

Yet sportswriters and fans have gotten Thorpe's greatness right. Jim Thorpe remains one of the most versatile athletes to have ever lived. As if being an Olympic champion were not enough, Thorpe returned from the 1912 Olympic games to dominate the sport of football. He was recognized as an All-American in both collegiate and professional football. He also played major-league baseball. In addition to these sports, Thorpe played basketball, lacrosse, tennis, and handball. His bowling scores averaged in the 200s and his golf scores were in the 70s.[6] Thorpe was also an excellent swimmer and a good billiards player. Other activities that Thorpe engaged in were boxing, archery, canoeing, and skating. Thorpe was also an excellent marksman, hunter, and fisherman. He was even a good dancer. He won an intercollegiate ballroom dancing championship—the Two-Step—with Clemce La Traille.[7]

During a difficult time in his life, Thorpe wondered about his Native American name of "Bright Path." He said, "I cannot decide whether I was well named or not. Many a time the path has gleamed bright for me, but just as often it has been dark and bitter indeed."[8]

To sports fans, the path of Jim Thorpe has indeed gleamed bright. He demonstrated an athletic greatness and versatility that has stood the test of time. Certainly he will be remembered as a legendary athlete for all centuries.

⋙⋙ CHRONOLOGY ⋘⋘

1888 ◈ Jim Thorpe is born on May 28.

1894 ◈ Thorpe attends Sac and Fox Agency School.

1896 ◈ Thorpe's twin brother, Charlie, dies from pneumonia.

1898 ◈ Thorpe enrolls at Haskell in Kansas; sees his first football game.

1901 ◈ Thorpe runs away to Texas; returns to attend Garden Grove school.

1904 ◈ Thorpe enrolls in Carlisle Indian School in Pennsylvania; in first school outing works on Buckholz farm.

1905 ◈ Thorpe works on Cadwallader farm and Rozarth farm.

1907 ◈ Thorpe returns to Carlisle from outings; joins track team and then football team.

1908 ◈ Thorpe wins five gold medals in track meet against Syracuse.

1909 ❖ Thorpe wins five gold medals in track meet against Lafayette; repeats 1908 five gold-medal performance against Syracuse track team; plays minor-league baseball for Rocky Mount, North Carolina, team.

1910 ❖ Thorpe plays minor-league baseball for Fayetteville, North Carolina, team.

1911 ❖ Thorpe returns to Carlisle school; plays outstanding football game against Harvard; is selected as first-team All-American halfback.

1912 ❖ Thorpe uses Carlisle track season to train for Olympic games; wins gold medals for pentathlon and decathlon; also takes fourth place in high jump and seventh place in long jump Olympic events; wins AAU All-Around Championship in Queens, New York; plays outstanding football game for Carlisle against Army, again is selected as first team All-American.

1913 ❖ Thorpe is stripped of Olympic gold medals and records; signs contract to play major-league baseball with New York Giants; marries Iva Miller.

1915 ❖ Thorpe's first son, James Jr., is born. Thorpe begins playing professional football with Canton, Ohio, Bulldogs.

1918 ❖ James Jr. dies from infantile paralysis.

1919 ❖ Thorpe has dispute with manager; major-league baseball career ends; continues to play minor-league baseball and professional football.

1920 ❖ Thorpe is elected president of American Professional Football Association (APFA), later to become National Football League (NFL).

1922 ❖ Thorpe plays with Oorang Indians football team.

1923 ❖ Thorpe and Iva Miller divorce.

1925 ❖ Thorpe marries Freeda Kirkpatrick; "officially" retires from sports.

1929 ❖ Thorpe sells movie rights to life story to MGM.

1930 ❖ Thorpe begins first of various jobs during Depression years.

1932 ❖ Thorpe attends Olympic games in Los Angeles, California, as guest of Vice President Curtis; receives standing ovation from crowd.

1937 ❖ Thorpe returns to Oklahoma to try to pass Wheeler bill, which is intended to help Native Americans gain more control over their lives.

1941 ◈ Thorpe and Freeda Kirkpatrick divorce.

1942 ◈ Thorpe begins work with security staff in March at Ford's River Rouge Plant in Dearborn, Michigan.

1943 ◈ Thorpe suffers first heart attack in February.

1945 ◈ Thorpe marries Patricia Gladys Askew; is assigned to duty with merchant marine.

1948 ◈ Thorpe is honored at football game between San Francisco 49ers and Baltimore Colts; trains Israeli National Soccer team.

1949 ◈ MGM sells movie rights to Thorpe's life story to Warner.

1950 ◈ Thorpe is voted "Greatest Football Player of the Half-Century" as well as "Best Male Athlete of Half a Century"

1951 ◈ Thorpe is voted into the College Football Hall of Fame and the Helms Hall Professional Football Hall of Fame; attends premiere of *Jim Thorpe—All-American* on August 23; is diagnosed with lip cancer in November.

1952 ◈ Thorpe suffers second heart attack in September.

1953 ◈ Thorpe suffers third, and fatal, heart attack on March 28.

1957 ❖ Thorpe's mausoleum in Jim Thorpe, Pennsylvania, is dedicated.

1963 ❖ Thorpe is inducted as a charter member of the Professional Football Hall of Fame in Canton, Ohio.

1969 ❖ Over five thousand signatures are collected on a petition asking for the return of Thorpe's gold medals and sent to the United States Olympic Committee.

1973 ❖ AAU restores amateur status to Thorpe for 1909-1912 period.

1982 ❖ IOC reinstates Thorpe's Olympic records and medals.

1983 ❖ Thorpe's children are presented with father's Olympic gold medals.

1984 ❖ Runners, including Thorpe's grandson Bill Jr., participate in "The Great Jim Thorpe Longest Run," a cross-country relay of the Olympic torch.

1996 ❖ Torch relay for 1996 Summer Olympics travels through Prague, Oklahoma— Thorpe's birthplace.

CHAPTER NOTES

Chapter 1

1. "Americans Lead All in Olympics," *The New York Times*, July 7, 1912, p. 1.

2. All 1912 Olympic statistics are taken from David Wallechinsky, *The Complete Book of the Olympics* (New York: Penguin Books, 1984).

3. "Americans Capture First Olympic Race," *The New York Times*, July 8, 1912, p. 1.

4. Wallechinsky, p. 107.

5. Robert W. Wheeler, *Jim Thorpe: World's Greatest Athlete* (Norman, Okla.: University of Oklahoma Press, 1979), p. 112.

6. William R. Sanford and Carl R. Green, *Jim Thorpe* (New York: Crestwood House, 1992), p. 22.

Chapter 2

1. Frederick J. Dockstader, *Great North American Indians: Profiles in Life and Leadership* (New York: Van Nostrand Reinhold Co., 1977), p. 35.

2. *The World Book Encyclopedia*, Volume 10 (Chicago, Ill.: World Book, Inc., 1992), p. 180.

3. Dockstader, p. 35.

4. William R. Sanford and Carl R. Green, *Jim Thorpe* (New York: Crestwood House, 1992), p. 7.

5. Thomas Fall, *Jim Thorpe* (New York: Crowell, 1970), p. 1.

6. Robert Lipsyte, *Jim Thorpe: 20th Century Jock* (New York: HarperCollins Publishers, 1993), p. 14.

7. William J. Gobrecht, *Jim Thorpe, Carlisle Indian* (Carlisle, Penn.: Cumberland County Historical Society and Hamilton Library Association, 1969), p. 4.

8. Sanford and Green, p. 8.

9. Bob Bernotas, *Jim Thorpe: Sac and Fox Athlete* (New York: Chelsea House Publishers, 1992), p. 27.

10. Robert W. Wheeler, *Jim Thorpe: World's Greatest Athlete* (Norman, Okla.: University of Oklahoma Press, 1979), p. 10.

11. Wayne Coffey, *Jim Thorpe* (Woodbridge, Conn.: Blackbirch Press, Inc., 1993), p. 10.

12. Lipsyte, p. 11.

13. Ibid., p. 18.

14. Edward F. Rivinus, *American Indian Stories: Jim Thorpe*, illustrated by Bob Masheris (Milwaukee, Wis.: Raintree Publishers, 1990), p. 6.

15. Lipsyte, p. 19.

16. Ibid.

17. Wheeler, p. 44.

18. Bernotas, p. 29.

19. Wheeler, p. 14.

20. Bernotas, p. 29.

21. Ibid.

22. Ibid., p. 30.

23. Rivinus, p. 8.

24. Wheeler, p. 18.

25. Ibid.

26. Ibid.

Chapter 3

1. Robert Lipsyte, *Jim Thorpe: 20th Century Jock* (New York: HarperCollins Publishers, 1993), p. 30.

2. Bob Bernotas, *Jim Thorpe: Sac and Fox Athlete* (New York: Chelsea House Publishers, 1992), p. 33.

3. Lipsyte, p. 33.

4. Ibid., p. 34.

5. Ibid., p. 31.

6. William R. Sanford and Carl R. Green, *Jim Thorpe* (New York: Crestwood House, 1992), p. 13.

7. Robert W. Wheeler, *Jim Thorpe: World's Greatest Athlete* (Norman, Okla.: University of Oklahoma Press, 1979), p. 48.

8. Lipsyte, p. 36.

9. Wheeler, p. 35.

10. Allison Danzig, *Oh, How They Played the Game* (New York: The Macmillan Co., 1971), p. 149.

11. Wheeler, p. 35.

12. Danzig, p. 158.

13. Ibid.

14. Ibid., pp. 160-161.

15. Ibid., p. 160.

16. Bernotas, p. 44.

17. Ibid., p. 49.

18. Lipsyte, p. 42.

19. Bernotas, p. 49.

20. Ibid.

Chapter 4

1. Bob Bernotas, *Jim Thorpe: Sac and Fox Athlete* (New York: Chelsea House Publishers, 1992), p. 45.

2. Robert Lipsyte, *Jim Thorpe: 20th Century Jock* (New York: HarperCollins Publishers, 1993), p. 43.

3. Robert W. Wheeler, *Jim Thorpe: World's Greatest Athlete* (Norman, Okla.: University of Oklahoma Press, 1979), p. 55.

4. Lipsyte, p. 44.

5. Ibid.

6. Allison Danzig, *Oh, How They Played the Game* (New York: Macmillan Co., 1971), p. 169.

7. Bernotas, p. 47.

8. Ibid., p. 50.

9. Lipsyte, p. 51.

10. Danzig, p. 17.

11. Wheeler, pp. 73-74.

12. William R. Sanford and Carl R. Green, *Jim Thorpe* (New York: Crestwood House, 1992), p. 17.

13. Edward F. Rivinus, *American Indian Stories: Jim Thorpe*, illustrated by Bob Masheris (Milwaukee, Wis.: Raintree Publishers, 1990), p. 17.

14. Lipsyte, p. 56.

15. Wayne Coffey, *Jim Thorpe* (Woodbridge, Conn.: Blackbirch Press, Inc., 1993), p. 22.

16. William J. Gobrecht, *Jim Thorpe, Carlisle Indian* (Carlisle, Penn.: Cumberland Historical Society and Hamilton Library Association, 1969), p. 5.

17. "Thorpe's Four Field Goals Beat Harvard," *The New York Times,* November 12, 1911, p. C1.

18. Ibid.

19. Ibid.

20. William S. Jarrett, *Timetables of Sports History: Football* (New York: Facts on File, 1993), p. 3.

21. Coffey, p. 23.

22. Joseph D'O'Brian, "The Greatest Athlete in the World," *American Heritage*, July/August 1992, p. 95.

23. Mary Klaus, "Superstar Jim Thorpe Put Carlisle on Map," *The Patriot*, April 10, 1978, p. 13.

24. Lipsyte, p. 58.

25. Wheeler, p. 162.

26. Ibid., p. 98.

Chapter 5

1. Allen Guttmann, *The Olympics: A History of the Modern Games* (Chicago, Ill.: University of Illinois Press, 1992), p. 1.

2. Ibid., p. 2.

3. Ibid., p. 12.

4. Ibid., p. 33.

5. William R. Sanford and Carl R. Green, *Jim Thorpe* (New York: Crestwood House, 1992), p. 20.

6. "American Athletes Sail for Stockholm," *The New York Times*, June 15, 1912, p. 9.

7. Robert Lipsyte, *Jim Thorpe: 20th Century Jock* (New York: HarperCollins Publishers, 1993), p. 60.

8. Robert W. Wheeler, *Jim Thorpe: World's Greatest Athlete* (Norman, Okla.: University of Oklahoma Press, 1979), p. 100.

9. Lipsyte, p. 60.

10. Bernotas, p. 11.

11. Robert Lindsay, "Thorpe's Medals Returned," *The New York Times*, January 19, 1983, p. B13.

12. Lipsyte, p. 65.

13. Joseph D'O'Brian, "The Greatest Athlete in the World," *American Heritage*, July/August, p. 96.

14. "Olympic Champions Cheered and Dined," *The New York Times*, August 25, 1912, p. 4.

15. Ibid.

16. Wheeler, p. 118.

17. Lipsyte, p. 68.

18. Wheeler, p. 128.

19. "Thorpe's Indians Crush West Point," *The New York Times*, November 10, 1912, p. 11.

20. Ibid.

21. Ibid.

22. Ibid.

23. Sanford and Green, p. 6.

24. Wheeler, p. 135.

25. Edward F. Rivinus, *American Indian Stories: Jim Thorpe*, illustrated by Bob Masheris (Milwaukee, Wis.: Raintree Publishers, 1990, p. 20.

26. Wayne Coffey, *Jim Thorpe* (Woodbridge, Conn.: Blackbirch Press, Inc., 1993), p. 24.

27. Allison Danzig, *Oh, How They Played the Game* (New York: Macmillan Co., 1971), p. 157.

28. Wheeler, p. 198.

29. Bernotas, p. 67.

30. *Carlisle Evening Sentinel*, January 28, 1913, p. 2.

31. Lipsyte, p. 52.

32. Wheeler, p. viii.

33. Ibid., p. 146.

34. Bernotas, p. 71.

35. Sanford and Green, p. 25.

36. Ibid.

37. Lipsyte, p. 76.

38. D'O'Brian, p. 98.

Chapter 6

1. Robert Lipsyte, *Jim Thorpe: 20th Century Jock* (New York: HarperCollins Publishers, 1993), p. 78.

2. Ibid.

3. Bob Bernotas, *Jim Thorpe: Sac and Fox Athlete* (New York: Chelsea House Publishers, 1992), p. 73.

4. Joseph D'O'Brian, "The Greatest Athlete in the World," *American Heritage*, July/August 1992, p. 98.

5. William R. Sanford and Carl R. Green, *Jim Thorpe* (New York: Crestwood House, 1992), p. 27.

6. Lipsyte, p. 86.

7. Sanford and Green, p. 27.

8. Lipsyte, p. 80.

9. Bernotas, p. 76.

10. Ibid.

11. Ibid.

12. D'O'Brian, p. 98.

13. William S. Jarrett, *Timetables of Sports History: Football* (New York: Facts on File, 1993), p. 5.

14. Edward F. Rivinus, *American Indian Stories: Jim Thorpe*, illustrated by Bob Masheris (Milwaukee, Wis.: Raintree Publishers, 1990), p. 24.

15. Allison Danzig, *Oh, How They Played the Game* (New York: Macmillan Co., 1971), p. 307.

16. Ibid., p. 304.

17. Sanford and Green, p. 30.

18. Ibid.

19. Bernotas, p. 81.

20. Sanford and Green, p. 31.

21. Bernotas, p. 81.

22. Lipsyte, p. 88.

23. Ibid., p, 85.

24. William J. Gobrecht, *Jim Thorpe, Carlisle Indian* (Carlisle, Penn.: Cumberland County Historical Society and Hamilton Library Association, 1969), p. 10.

Chapter 7

1. William J. Gobrecht, *Jim Thorpe, Carlisle Indian* (Carlisle, Penn.: Cumberland County Historical Society and Hamilton Library Association, 1969), p. 11.

2. Allen Guttmann, *The Olympics: A History of the Modern Games* (Chicago, Ill.: University of Illinois Press, 1992), p. 50.

3. Robert W. Wheeler, *Jim Thorpe: World's Greatest Athlete* (Norman, Okla.: University of Oklahoma Press, 1979), p. 195.

4. Robert Lipsyte, *Jim Thorpe: 20th Century Jock* (New York: HarperCollins Publishers, 1993), p. 86.

5. Wheeler, p. 195.

6. Ibid., p. 196.

7. Ibid., p. 198.

8. Bob Bernotas, *Jim Thorpe: Sac and Fox Athlete* (New York: Chelsea House Publishers, 1992), p. 88.

9. Ibid., p. 90.

10. Wheeler, p. 207.

11. Bernotas, p. 92.

12. Wayne Coffey, *Jim Thorpe* (Woodbridge, Conn., Blackbirch Press, Inc., 1993), p. 6.

13. "Jim Thorpe Is Dead on West Coast at 64," *The New York Times*, March 29, 1953, p. 1.

Chapter 8

1. Robert W. Wheeler, *Pathway to Glory* (New York: Carlton Press, Inc., 1975), p. 236.

2. "Jim Thorpe Memorial Dedicated as 5,000 Hail 'Greatest Athlete,'" *The Morning Call*, May 31, 1957, pp. 5, 7.

3. Robert W. Wheeler, *Jim Thorpe: World's Greatest Athlete* (Norman, Okla.: University of Oklahoma Press, 1979), p. viii.

4. "Longest Marathon Ends for Thorpe," *The Times Record*, October 14, 1982, p. 14.

5. Jere Longman, "Torch Run Takes a Wrong Turn," *The New York Times*, December 9, 1995.

6. Wheeler, *Jim Thorpe: World's Greatest Athlete*, p. 141.

7. Ibid.

8. Bob Bernotas, *Jim Thorpe: Sac and Fox Athlete* (New York: Chelsea Publishers, 1992), p. 93.

Glossary

Airedale—A large terrier dog with a wiry, black-and-tan coat.

amateur athlete—A competitor who does not receive material gain for playing a sport.

Amateur Athletic Union (AAU)—The organization that governed amateur sports in the United States during Jim Thorpe's day.

blood poisoning—An invasion of bacteria, caused by infection, into the bloodstream; its symptoms include chills and fever; also called septicemia.

bust—A sculpture that represents the upper part of a person, including the head, neck, and shoulders.

center—A football playing position that is in the middle of the front line of players.

crypt—A chamber, or room, in a mausoleum.

◈ **decathlon**—A track competition that consists of the following ten events: 100-meter dash, long jump, shot put, high jump, 400-meter run, 110-meter hurdles, discus throw, pole vault, javelin throw, and 1,500-meter race.

◈ **devout**—Earnest or sincere; devoted.

◈ **divest**—Take away or deprive a person of property, authority, or title.

◈ **drop kick**—In football, a technique in which a player drops the ball on the ground and kicks it as it rebounds off the ground; in early football days, this technique was used to score field goals and extra points.

◈ **end zone**—An area at each end of a football field that extends from the goal line to the end line.

◈ **extra**—A person hired to act in a group scene of a movie or play.

◈ **field goal**—A football play in which a player kicks the ball through one of a set of goalposts located at each end of the field; if successful, the field goal results in a score for that player's team.

◈ **food poisoning**—A poisoning caused by bacteria.

◈ **guard**—A football playing position next to the center position on the front line of players.

❖ **halfback**—A football playing position behind the front line of players.

❖ **heart attack**—A very serious heart disease caused by insufficient blood supply to the heart due to a blocked artery; its symptoms include prolonged heavy pressure and pain; also called myocardial infarction.

❖ **impervious**—Unable to be harmed, injured, or damaged.

❖ **infantile paralysis**—A virus affecting the spinal cord; its symptoms include fever, headache, vomiting, and paralysis—or loss of the ability to move; also called poliomyelitis.

❖ **interception**—In football, a play in which a defensive player catches a pass intended for an offensive player.

❖ **International Olympic Committee (IOC)**—The organization that governs the Olympic games; each participating country has its own Olympic committee, but these committees must follow the general IOC rules.

❖ **intramural team**—A competitive group made up of members of a particular institution, organization, or community.

◈ **irony**—A literary term that refers to an idea or statement that displays a difference between the actual outcome of an event and the expected outcome of an event.

◈ **linemen**—Football players positioned on the front line.

◈ **merchant marine**—The privately or publicly owned commercial ships of a country.

◈ **mausoleum**—A large tomb, usually of stone.

◈ **orthodox**—Conventional.

◈ **outing**—A program at the Carlisle Indian School during which Native Americans spent time away from the school and with white families to learn various skills as well as white customs.

◈ **pentathlon**—A track competition that consists of the following five events: long jump, javelin throw, 200-meter race, discus throw, and 1,500-meter race; is now an event in the Olympic games.

◈ **pneumonia**—An inflammation of the lungs, caused by bacteria, viruses, or chemical irritants; symptoms include fever, chills, coughing, and chest pain.

◈ **powerhouse**—A sports team that has great ability and strength.

◈ **premiere**—A first performance, showing, or exhibition.

◈ **professional athlete**—A competitor who receives material gain for playing a sport.

◈ **promoter**—A person who profits, or attempts to profit, from organizing a paid athletic event.

◈ **prowess**—Extraordinary ability or skill.

◈ **punt**—A football technique in which a player drops the ball and kicks it before it reaches the ground.

◈ **quarterback**—A football playing position behind the center; this player calls and begins the plays.

◈ **reservation**—Land set aside for use by Native Americans.

◈ **Rosary**—A Roman Catholic devotion that consists of meditation on five sacred religious mysteries; beads that are used as memory and concentration aids while praying the Rosary.

◈ **send-off**—An enthusiastic demonstration of goodwill for the beginning of a trip or venture.

◈ **stoicism**—Indifference to pleasure or pain.

◈ **ticker-tape parade**—A festive procession in which small bits of paper are dropped on the parading celebrities.

◈ **touchdown**—A football play in which a player carries the football across the goal line before being tackled, resulting in a score; a player may also catch the ball in the end zone for a score.

◈ **trade**—An occupation, industry, or business.

◈ **Victorian**—Relating to the 1837-1901 period in which Queen Victoria ruled England.

FURTHER READING

Bernotas, Bob. *Jim Thorpe: Sac and Fox Athlete*. New York: Chelsea House Publishers, 1992.

Coffey, Wayne. *Jim Thorpe*. Woodbridge, CT: Blackbirch Press, Inc., 1993.

Danzig, Allison. *Oh, How They Played the Game*. New York: The Macmillan Co., 1971.

D'O'Brian, Joseph. "The Greatest Athlete in the World." *American Heritage*. July/August, 1992.

Dockstader, Frederick J. *Great North American Indians: Profiles in Life and Leadership*. New York: Van Nostrand Reinhold Co., 1977.

Fall, Thomas. *Jim Thorpe*. New York: Crowell, 1970.

Gobrecht, William J. *Jim Thorpe, Carlisle Indian*. Carlisle, PA: Cumberland County Historical Society and Hamilton Library Association, 1969.

Guttmann, Allen. *The Olympics: A History of the Modern Games.* Chicago, IL: University of Illinois Press, 1992.

Jarrett, William S. *Timetables of Sports History: Football.* New York: Facts on File, 1993.

Lipsyte, Robert. *Jim Thorpe: 20th Century Jock.* New York: HarperCollins Publishers, 1993.

Nardo, Don. *Jim Thorpe.* San Diego, CA: Lucent Books, 1994.

Newcombe, Jack. *The Best of the Athletic Boys.* New York: Doubleday, 1975.

Rasmussen, Della Mae. *Power of Sportsmanship.* Antioch, CA: Eagle Systems International Publications, 1981.

Reising, Robert. *Jim Thorpe.* Minneapolis, MN: Dillon Press, 1974.

Richards, Gregory. *Jim Thorpe: World's Greatest Athlete.* Chicago, IL: Children's Press, 1984.

Rivinus, Edward F., illustrated by Bob Masheris. *American Indian Stories: Jim Thorpe.* Milwaukee, WI: Raintree Publishers, 1990.

Sanford, William R., and Carl R. Green. *Jim Thorpe.* New York: Crestwood House, 1992.

Steiger, Brad, and Charlotte Thorpe. *Thorpe's Gold.* New York: Dee/Quicksilver, 1984.

Wallechinsky, David. *The Complete Book of the Olympics*, Boston, MA: Little, Brown and Company, 1992.

Wheeler, Robert W. *Jim Thorpe: World's Greatest Athlete.* Norman, OK: University of Oklahoma Press, 1979.

―――. *Pathway to Glory.* New York: Carlton Press, Inc., 1975.

INDEX